KHADIJAH

A Thank You To Ya!

MARK BROOKS

Author's Other Works

About The ~~Author~~ Special Person
This Book Is Written For

This is where I'm supposed to tell you a bit about me and being from Wolverhampton etc. etc but let's face it you haven't picked this book up to read about this idiot, no, no, no, you don't want to read about me so let's introduce you to the person the book is dedicated to, the reason you've picked up this book, – Khadijah.

This beautiful, special, amazing lady blessed my life with her presence in February this year, (2023) and instantly I just felt I could talk to her about anything and everything and be like an open book with her, I just felt so comfortable talking to her about stuff I don't or can't usually talk about, personal stuff, feelings, emotions etc.

It's strange, it's a strange feeling, but I feel like I have known her forever. I wish I had known her for longer but even if I'd known her forever, I'd still wish it was longer.

This special amazing person has the biggest, most sweetest, most beautiful heart, she's the most selfless person I have ever met, she's amazing. Khadijah always puts others first including this idiot no matter how busy she is or how much she has on her plate to deal with she is always concerned about others first. Khadijah knows when I'm down and low and even when she should be focusing on herself she orders that I talk to her and tell her what's going on, she listens, she counsels, she always helps me see things with clarity and perspective and always makes me smile everyday, she's the reason I smile everyday, it's strange but around her I feel happy all the time, she's truly gifted, she always makes me feel lifted. Khadijah always knows when I'm off colour and not myself, she knows me better than I know me.

Yes, when life is dark and gloomy, Khadijah is the light, she's the sunshine, In my world she makes the sun shine everyday, she brightens up my life making everyday bright and fun.

Khadijah and I have had some laughs together as you will see from the poems inside this book, we have a fun, quirky, unique friendship as the poems will tell you so what are you waiting for, don't just listen to me, start reading and discover for yourself how amazing and special this lady is as the poems give you an insight into our quirky friendship and the fun and laughs we have had together and poems inspired by our friendship and memories of the magic moments spent in her company and here's hoping we have many, many more chapters together in this wonderful, beautiful, unique, quirky friendship of ours yet to be written.

So please, read on and see for yourself and I'm sure at the other end of this book you'll agree and say wow, this lady sure does sound amazing, special and so much more and will probably, no definitely leave you thinking, damn, I wish I knew her, I wish I had a friend like her.

FOREWORD

Hello and thank you for purchasing this book. I hope you enjoy reading it and discovering all about the amazing lady this book is written for and dedicated to – Khadijah.

This book is a thank you to her for everything she does for me, always looking out for me, making me laugh and smile, being there to talk to about anything and everything. Thanking her for all the magical moments spent with her in her company.

These poems are inspired by our fun, wonderfully quirky friendship, you will see from the poems inside the book the quirky nature of our friendship, the laughs we have, the fun, the magic moments spent in her company and hopefully the poems explains the bond we have how we look out for one another and are there for each other, having each others backs like friends do.

So please read on and discover for yourselves how truly amazing this special lady is.

Thank you for choosing to read this book and I wish you all lots of love and happiness.

Mark xx

<u>Dedication</u>

Khadijah – A Thank You To Ya! Is dedicated to a truly amazing, special lady, Khadijah.

Khadijah, this book is a thank you to you, a thank you for everything that you do, how you always look out for me, how you always check on me, make me smile and laugh everyday, how you light up my world and make everyday bright.

It's a thank you for all the magical moments spent in your company, all the chats we've had and for all the times you've picked me up when I've been low, down and out.

You know I think the absolute world of you buddy, I hope this book of poems shows you how much I love and cherish our friendship as the poems recall some of the magic moments in our friendship, hopefully as you read these poems they make you smile, they make you laugh, hopefully not cry (though I'll admit this softy did when writing some of them) but this book is a huge thank you to you for blessing me with your presence in my life.

Khadijah, Thank you for everything, my dear, special, amazing friend.

Never lose your beautiful, bright smile buddy and keep shining bright like the star you are, thank you for everything and I hope you enjoy the book.

Here's to making many, many more memories together in our wonderfully quirky friendship and writing many, many more chapters filled with lots of laughs and fun – and more me "cracking you up".

Never change buddy, because you're amazing just the way you are.

Thank you Khadijah.

Love

Mark (Jack)

xxx

Acknowledgements

Only one place to start with the acknowledgements and that is to acknowledge the amazing, special lady that this poetry collection is written for and dedicated to, Khadijah.

Thank you buddy, for everything, making me laugh and smile, being there through good times and bad, all the magic moments spent together in your company and all the memories we've made.

Thank you for always making me smile everyday, being the reason I smile everyday, thank you for looking out for me, checking on me, thank you for just being there.

I'd like to thank my friend James Robins (artist and author) for the fantastic cover to the book, making the idea a reality. Thanks mate.

Of course, a big thank you to you, all the readers and those of you who have purchased this book and I hope you enjoy reading it and learning all about this beautiful, special, amazing lady, my dear friend, Khadijah.

It seems only fitting that we should finish the acknowledgements the way we started, with the special lady the book is dedicated to, Khadijah, so Khadijah, buddy, thank you again for everything, I sincerely hope you enjoy the book and it makes you smile and laugh and shows you how lucky I am to be blessed with an amazing friend like you. I hope the book shows you how special you are.

Thank you again Khadijah.

.

KHADIJAH

A Thank You To Ya!

Contents

Thank You

No. 1

Khadijah, I'm not going to do a long introduction to this poem, I could never express enough words, so I'm sorry it will just be these two words …. Thank You.

Somehow it doesn't seem enough for everything you've done for me, and you'll probably never know or understand just how much you have helped me and made a difference to my life. You are amazing, the loveliest, kindest human I have ever, ever met, the sweetest soul and the biggest of hearts, you're a special person Khadijah I hope you know that. What a wonderful world (oops sorry song lyrics again but you know me by now) lol, as I was saying, what a wonderful world this would be if there were more you's in this world.

Apologies, that was longer than I anticipated but I could have waxed lyrical about you for ages how amazing you are.

I thought I would do something different,

something original,

Not flowers or chocolates or that kind of

traditional,

No, something special,

Hope it makes you smile,

I haven't wrote this many poems in a long while,

Just wanted to do something to say thanks,

Hopefully you don't think this book is pants,

Just hope you like it,

The poems have it all, seriousness but also

humour and wit,

Hopefully it will stand the test of time,

Future generations will know how special and

wonderful Khadijah was/is, this friend of mine,

Long after you and I are gone,

Hopefully with this book, your name will always

live on,

Forever,

Forgotten never,

Hopefully reading this about you,

Future generations will say, God, her, I wish I

knew,

So this book is especially for you,

To say thank you for everything you do,

How you look out for me, I appreciate that too,

You've been such a good friend,

I can't pretend,

If it wasn't for you,

These past couple of months, I don't think I

would have made it through,

But for me you've been there,

To talk too, my thoughts, my feelings, share,

I just feel so comfortable with you,

It's like forever, you, I have knew,

I can be like an open book,

And look,

You've done all this whilst being so busy,

Yet never once have you complained, always

finding time for me,

Never once telling me to piss off,

Or get lost,

Thank you for making me feel worthwhile,

Thank you everyday, for being the reason I smile,

Thank you for the lunchtimes out and the silly

games we play,

Thank you for being the reason I look forward to
each working day,
Thank you for all the checking ins,
Thank you for making sure I've had breakfast and
din dins,
Thank you for all the pep talks,
Thank you for picking me up when I'm low and
on the floor,
Thank you for all the compliments,
Thank you for the boosts in confidence,
For everything, just thank you,
For everything you do,
One more time from me,
To thee,
Thank you,
For everything you do,
My beautiful, wonderful, special amazing friend,
Khadijah,
Here's a toast to ya, and once again I thank ya!

I Wrote You A Book!

No. 2

Khadijah, I wrote you a book, I just wanted to put in words my gratitude to you hopefully saying all the things that if I tried to tell you in person I'd get all muddled up and sound like an even bigger idiot than I already am. It's a collection of poems ranging from thanks and praise to remembering some of the fun times together and laughs we've had and basically just our friendship, well you'll see for yourself hopefully if you read this. I hope the book makes you laugh more than cry. A couple of the poems I got emotional when writing them but shush don't tell anyone because big boys don't cry apparently.

You know me matey,

Silly, stupid me,

Useless at serious talking,

If I tried that with this, I'd just sound like an idiot

rambling,

So thought what the hell, this probably says it

more than flowers,

So thought I'd put in the time, put in the hours,

See if I can somehow put some words together,

To try and tell ya what I'd probably screw up if I
tried to tell you in person Khadijah,
So I wrote you this,
That you like it and that it says it all is my only
wish,
Khadijah, this is a collection of poem after poem,
Written for you with the intention of, you, my
thanks showing,
I know you're down to earth and modest,
But to know you and call you a friend, I'm truly
blessed,
So this is going to be a book that's going to do a
lot of praising,
Because I think you're amazing,
So please read on at your leisure,
I do hope it makes you smile and brings you
some pleasure,
Especially for you my beautiful dear friend
Khadijah.

For Your Eyes Only

No. 3

Khadijah, I've not shared any of these with anyone but you now, I thought as they are personal between you and me, of course if you wanted to share them with friends, family, by all means after all they are your poems, written especially for you. I just wanted you to know how amazing I think you are, how thankful I am to you for always checking on me and seeing how I am doing despite having so much on your own plate, your revision, your exam etc, and how you've always found time for me to talk to and never told me to piss off or said you're too busy even though you are, I've told you a million times, you're the loveliest most selfless human I have ever met always putting others first so anyway stop rambling Mark, so anyway mate just wanted to do something special for you, so I wrote you a book which I hope covers everything I want to say and expresses my gratitude and admiration for you.

For your eyes only,

Hey isn't that a title of a Bond movie?

Guess that makes you the Bond girl,

Only you're more special and beautiful,

A book written for and dedicated to you, I

thought it'd be a personal touch,

A way of me saying thank you very much,

A way of saying I care,

And thank you for just being there,

As you read on, (hopefully!), you'll see a good

mix,

Poems both serious and full of wit,

Poems of times spent in each others company,

Poems personal to just you and me,

Poems just for your eyes only.

To Be Read After Your Exam …

No. 4

Khadijah, obviously I can't tell you what to do, I can't tell you not to read it until after your exam but I don't want this book to be a distraction before your exam and take you away from your revision or preparation but hopefully will be something to look forward to after your exam is done, something for you to read, hopefully you like it, hopefully you enjoy it.

I don't want this to serve as a distraction,

That's not my intention,

It's why the book comes with that instruction,

To be read after you've done all your revision,

And at the exams conclusion,

I don't want anything getting in the way of your

preparation,

Hopefully it might serve as a way of relaxation,

Come post examination.

Legacy (You'll Be Remembered)

No. 5

Khadijah, for once I haven't or am not going to say a lot here, no real need to. I guess/hope the title says it all and the poem too.

You'll always, always matter matey, and with this book of poems and with your star shining bright up in a galaxy far, far, away you will never ever, ever be forgotten, you'll never be a faded memory, you will live on, these poems, this book, your star will always be here for all eternity, long after we're gone people will always be able to read about what an amazing, truly special person you were and when they see your star illuminating and brightening the dark night sky they'll say there she is, that wonderful amazing Khadijah, watching over us.

You know how I've told you before if we ever drift apart how I'll always be looking to your star and somehow would still feel close to you and that I could still somehow talk to you and I've told you before and multiple times how special you are and how I think the world of you and will never ever forget you.

Yep matey, you're important, you're special, you matter and always will and will never be forgotten and will never ever be a mere faded memory.

This book, the star, ensures you'll live forever.

A hundred years from now,

I'll doubt I'll still be here somehow,

Nothing left to remember me,

But not thee,

This book of poems will be a legacy,

Ensure that you will never just be a faded, distant

memory,

Ensuring that forever,

You, people will always remember,

Generations young and old,

Will be told,

When they read this and get to know ya,

They'll read all about this beautiful, bright

amazing woman called Khadijah,

And this book, through,

They will always know how you were the most

amazing, special human that I ever knew,

Yep, a hundred years from now after you and I

are long gone,

Hopefully through this book you'll forever live

on,

And people will read just how special you were,

My beautiful, amazing, special friend, Khadijah,

This collection of poetry,

A legacy,

Ensuring that a hundred years from now you'll

live on in the memory.

Khadijah

No. 6

Apologies to anyone reading this if I upset or offend anyone by getting some information wrong as I (hopefully not foolishly relied on Google for researching some of this – hope it hasn't mislead me).

Khadijah, what a beautiful name.

Khadijah, I've always called you by your full name as it's a respect thing – you know how much I respect you buddy, I remember you saying you preferred people call you Khadijah instead of shortening your name to Kay or Khad or anything else and Khadijah really isn't that hard to say after all is it?

I remember one of our many, many chats, this particular one I refer to was when you was telling me about your name and what it meant, I remember you asked me if I knew what it meant. I had said trustworthy, reliable as I had looked into it and that's what google had said but I wasn't sure if it was accurate. You know, and I've told you many times, I love learning something new about you, I'm always fascinated by what you say, by you, you speak, I always listen intently because you know I think you're amazing so I am always truly honoured whenever you share something with me about you, I love learning new things about you. I'm doing what I always do and going off-piste again, anyway we was in your office talking about your name and you brought it up on your computer and was a little surprised when it come up saying early baby.

Google when researching also mentioned trustworthy and respect, both qualities of which definitely suit your personality and name, I mean as I've touched on, you know I have nothing but the utmost adulation and respect for you matey, you know how much I respect you, you know anything you tell me, never goes further because I'm honoured that you share these things with me and clearly feel comfortable doing so and for that honour I thank you dearly.

Trustworthy, well I needn't say anything about this I've said it countless times in this book alone but yep, I trust you completely, I trust you with everything and anything, I can talk to you about anything, I can be like an open book with you, I'd trust you with my life, I just trust you. You know it's a big thing for me to trust someone, I find it hard, but not with you, not with you I didn't, it was instant, I just felt like I'd known you forever and could talk to you openly from day one, that's huge for me, you know this already but you're clearly very, very special. The sweetest, kindest human I've ever been lucky enough to meet.

Yep and Khadijah's also make others feel comfortable and happy and are exemplary friends. Well how many times have I told you how you're the most selfless person I know always putting others first before yourself to make sure others are okay including this idiot more than once. Revising for your exam and your busy life but despite all this you'd still ask how I am and if I was down you'd summon me to your office like a naughty schoolboy to the headmistress order me to sit down and talk even when I'd say no, you've got your own important stuff to do like your revision etc. without worrying about this idiot but being the amazing, kind, sweet, selfless person that you are, you insisted and listen, counsel, advise and make me see things with clarity and perspective, yep you always put others before you matey, and I've told you how important you are, you're important too matey and I hope you know, please know, that I'm always, always, always here for you too buddy, any time, any place, I promise.

Khadijah's are also ambitious and I know how hard you work, how hard you have worked to get this far and how driven you are too. You're amazing, and I hope I've helped during your revision for your exam keeping you encouraged telling you how I believe in you and have faith in you, you're brilliant, you're going to pass this exam and you are going to go far, you're a star, you're so bright and clever, there is nothing you can't achieve matey, nothing and I promise you, whatever you do, I'll always support and encourage you and always by your side, on your side and always got your back forever buddy.

And now the main point, in your culture and faith, no woman is more important than Khadijah, and again you know how important you are to me, you are in my life, you know how much and how highly I value you, at least I hope you do, seriously, you're probably, no, no probably about it, you're the most important female figure in my life buddy. You know how you are always the first person I want to tell things to and share things with, I value and trust you that much buddy.

This is where I hope my research by Google doesn't let me down as I don't want to get it wrong so apologies to you and anyone reading this that might get offended if my research is wrong, that of course wasn't my intention.

I hope it's right Khadijah.

Khadijah was the wife of the Prophet Muhammad and the mother of his children. They had six children, two boys and four girls. Sadly neither the two boys, Qasim and Abdullah survived infancy. The four daughters were Zainab, Ruqayya, Umm Kulthum and Fatimah.

Khadijah, according to the Prophet (Saw) was

one of the four greatest women among the whole earth.

Khadijah was and continues to be a role model to the followers of the Muslim faith.

Born in 555C.E she was a very successful merchant and had attained quite a reputation for herself as a fine natured business woman by the time she was 40 years old.

Khadijah entrusted Nafisa to approach Muhammad to ascertain if he would consider marriage, Muhammad had hesitated, worried that he hadn't the means to support a wife when it was proposed would he consider marriage to a woman who had means to provide for herself and after meeting, their respective Uncles agreed to the marriage and the marriage took place. Khadijah was approximately fifteen years older than Muhammad.

Muhammad would often go to Mount Hira (some research says it was a cave) It was on returning from one of these trips that Muhammad returned home to Khadijah in a state of terror asking to be covered with a blanket and after calming down he described his experience to Khadijah who comforted him with the words that Allah would surely protect him from any danger, and would never allow anyone to revile him as he was a man of peace and reconciliation and always extended the hand of friendship to all. Shortly after this it was Khadijah's cousin Waraqah Ibn Nawfal that confirmed Muhammad's Prophethood.

Khadijah was supportive of Muhammad's prophetic mission, always helping in his work, proclaiming his message and belittling any opposition to his prophecies. It was her encouragement that helped Muhammad believe in his mission and spread Islam. Khadijah also invested her wealth in the mission. When the <u>polytheists</u> and aristocrats of the Quraysh harassed the Muslims, she used her money to ransom Muslim slaves and feed the Muslim community. She was also content to raise the children and handle the family affairs so that Muhammad could preach.

Khadijah remained Muhammad's only wife until her death in 620C.E aged 65 and long after her death, Muhammad remembered and honoured her often.

Khadijah, I suppose I better get on with the poem now but hopefully the above is factual and I haven't read the wrong thing when researching as I'd hate to offend you or anybody else reading this with wrong information and sincere apologies if I've gotten it wrong. Google, I'm trusting you not to have let me down.

.

Khadijah,

Not that hard to say eh?

I always call you by your proper name,

For others, I cannot say the same,

For short, some call you Khad or Kay,

Is Khadijah really that hard to say?

Khadijah is to you, what I refer,

As when we met that's what you said you prefer,

It's a respect thing,

And your name pronunciation is hardly taxing,

Your name is beautiful,

In your faith, your name is special,

I hope Google hasn't let me down with the
research,

Last thing I want to do with your sacred name is
to it, besmirch,

I hope Google don't leave me looking like a total
complete berk,

Come on Google, please don't let me down,

And leave me looking like an ass clown,

Sincerest apologies if I get anything incorrect,

I sincerely hope I don't as you know for you I
have nothing but adulation and respect,
Khadijah, according to Google it says it means
early baby,
But I've also found "respect" and "trustworthy",
Both of which would suit your personality,
You know I have the utmost respect for you,
And you know how I trust you implicitly, you
know I trust very few people like I trust you, I do,
It also states that Khadijah's make friends that as
friends are exemplary,
You're an amazing friend, so no arguments from
me,
I completely agree,
They also try hard to make sure everyone is
comfortable and happy,
See, I pointed out that your kind, sweet and
selfless you are always thinking of others first and
this is your special quality,
It also states about being ambitious I now how
hard you work and how driven you are,

And trust me, you're going to go far,

You're a superstar,

In your culture and religion,

Khadijah, was the most important woman,

And again, your name seems so apt,

Because of how important you are to me, in my

life, ... Fact!

Good Luck In Your Exam

No. 7

Khadijah, you've already seen this poem but thought I would put it in here too. I should thank you as this was only my second poem I had written this year until these others in the book too, so thank you for giving me a reason to get back into my writing.

Good luck in your exam mate, you're going to do great, but if ever you need a confidence boost or have any doubts on whether you can do this, hopefully this will make you smile and give you a bit of encouragement and tell you that you are great and that I believe in you for what it's worth.

Ah, Here goes,

How it will turn out, God only knows!

I'm out of practice,

So lets see how I get on with this,

Only my second poem of the year,

That it's no good is my biggest fear,

Hopefully it will bring you some cheer,

Hoping that it turns out alright,

Hoping that you don't think it's s%!#e,

That when you wonder is all this studying
worthwhile,

That you read this and smile,

I hadn't planned on doing this until closer to your
exam date,

But thought you might have needed to hear that
you're great!

But just wanted to wish you luck and tell you,
you've got this mate!

Thought I'd write something in case you needed a
confidence boost for the final big push,

Before your exam in August,

If those doubts creep in saying I can't do this
man,

Have faith in the words of George Michael of
wham,

Read this again and see that YOU CAN!

You can, therefore you will!

You're such an intelligent girl,

You've worked so hard and come so far, so don't
stop,

It's almost time to collect the pay off,

You should be proud of yourself, you've done

amazing,

I know it hasn't all been plain sailing,

Bless you, you've had it rough,

With more than your fair share of bad luck,

But you should be proud of all you've come

through, you're made of tough stuff,

Lesser people would have given up,

But knowing you for only a short time, already I

know that's not you,

Giving up just isn't what you do.

And I believe in you too!

In the words of Billy Ocean when the going gets

tough the tough get going,

And that's you, always persevering,

No matter what, at you, life keeps throwing,

No matter how many times life makes you fall,

Each time you get up stronger than before,

Standing proud and tall,

You're an inspiration,

How you seemingly come through each trial and

tribulation,

Testament to your character,

You never let anything get the better of ya,

Something to admire,

Which is why I know you are going to go far,

You're going to shine bright like a star,

If I could,

I would,

Would help you with your study,

But best not rely on me, I'm a dummy!

But you, you're brainy,

So you'll be more than fine,

Trust me, I know it, I feel it in this heart of mine,

I allegedly have one somewhere,

(Pointing at his chest) In there,

No, I'm afraid supplying you with brain power

foods full of energy,

Such as biscuits and Jaffa cakes is the best use I

can offer from me,

Sorry!

Khadijah,

You won't need no lucky horseshoe, rabbits foot

or four leaf clover,

You're so clever,

There's nothing for you to fear,

You should be confident,

Because you're brilliant,

So go and kick ass,

The exam, you'll smash,

And you'll bring back that pass!

And Khadijah,

That's not a prediction it's a spoiler!

And when you're big time,

And you need an assistant, remember I'm first in

line,

Typing, filing, making tea,

You name it, but remember ME!

When you're looking for your assistant,

remember the words of our old friend, (yes it's

him again!) George Michael of Wham,

Then, I'm your man!

But seriously, I know these words won't get you

any extra marks on your test paper,

But they're for mere encouragement and to let

you know I'm behind ya!

I believe in you,

There's nothing you can't do if you just believe in

you too!

You can read these words again if you ever need a

pick me up,

But Khadijah, wishing you success in your exam

and the best of luck,

That better be all from me,

So you can get back to your books and study!

Good luck in you're exam mate,

Go smash,

Get that pass,

You're gonna do just great.

Good Luck Bear

No. 8

Khadijah, just a poem about our little Twix, hopefully he brings you good luck in your exam, hopefully he helps you get through your revision, inspires you to keep going and tells you, you can do this if the doubts begin to creep in. If you're studying and revising and think you can't do this, you'll see little Twix, and think of me too and know that I believe in you, I know you can and I know you WILL do this. You're so clever Khadijah, you can do it, you've worked so hard and come through so much, what you've come through and still carried on, lesser people, would have given up but not you Khadijah, you're determined, you're strong, you're brave, you're amazing, you're inspirational, you haven't come this far to only come this far so from me and our little bear Twix, good luck in your exam buddy, go smash it, you're brilliant!

I won't ever forget the story of why you called him Twix, it really touched me matey, I thought it was lovely and sweet. I remember you telling me you called him Twix, you said well like Jack and Rose, we're a team and I thought Twix because left Twix to my Right Twix. Yeah, yeah I'll always be on your side I promise, I've got your back and I'll always will have matey. It's crazy but I felt like I've known you forever buddy, it's only a few short months but I feel like I've always known you, I just feel so comfortable with you I'd be lost without you in my life now matey. And now we've always got a tie to each other now ain't we with little Twix. Lol.

A little bear, small and cuddly,

To you from me,

To act as a keep going, you got this mascot as you

study,

Hopefully proving to be lucky,

It made me smile as you said you called him

Twix,

As with his little t-shirt and four leaf clover, good

luck, you, he does wish,

I respond no Miss,

When, do you know why I called him this?

You did ask?

Do you know why I called him that?

Me, you did ask in our chat,

As you explained, remember me and you like Jack

and Rose?

Well, yeah, the left twix to my right twix aren't

you, we're a team, that's how it goes!

Hopefully if you're ever in need of inspiration,

To keep going in your revision,

When you think you can't do it and feeling in

desperation,

You see little Twix,

And he's smiling at you sweetly saying come on

Khadijah, you got this,

So with this little bear,

I hope I show you that I really, really do care,

As me and little Twix,

Send you this good luck wish,

Khadijah, you've got this,

Miss.

Our Friend George

No. 9

Khadijah, I feel bloody stupid with this poem, it's like there is bloody three of us in this one! Lol. Well you'll see from the way it's written with our friend George keep interrupting making reference to his songs lol.

Hopefully this will make you smile and laugh. We always talk about our friend George and what he would say. You know I believe in you matey and know you're going to smash this exam, I'm so proud of you matey, everything life has thrown at you and that's just in the short time I've known you and from our conversations, you're doing marvelous matey, you know how amazing I think you are. The way you never stop down after life keeps dealing you shit card after shit card, you keep getting up, you're an inspiration to me, so strong but you know I'm here for you matey if you ever need me for anything, to lean on, vent at, hit (not too hard though eh?) a shoulder to cry on, anything, after all, you've done that for me countless times. You're the most amazing woman I have met with the biggest most caring heart, honestly, the loveliest human I've ever met, I've told you that before though.

Yep so with everything that you've been through I totally understand when the doubts creep in and you say you can't do this exam, both me and our friend George are there to pick you up and say yes you can, yes you will, believe in yourself because you're brilliant, you gotta have faith! We always talk about this and have a laugh as we have said many a time, what would our friend George say? Well read this poem, he says a bloody lot! Lol. Interrupting and interfering. Lol and referencing his bloody songs, Faith, Club Tropicana, I'm Your Man, Everything She Wants and Amazing.

Anyway, hope you like this and find it funny.

We have a friend called George,

Whose full of many a wise word,

When you have doubts and exam nerves,

When you say I can't do this,

We can hear our friend George's voice,

He's saying listen Miss,

I'm gonna make myself heard,

Listen to my words,

Just like my song says, you gotta have faith,

In this exam you're gonna be ace,

And Khadijah, this may be wishful thinking,

But I'm sure I heard George singing,

As to you he says, and when you pass,

The exam, that you'll smash,

In the words of my song with Wham,

Khadijah, when you need an assistant when you

qualify, remember, Mark's your man!

For the recommendation, to George, I say thank

you,

To serve Khadijah, I'd love to,

To be part of Team Khadijah,

I'd promise her that I would not fail her,

Wait, what's that, George what did you say?

George says when the exam is over we'll have to

go out and celebrate some way,

Sorry mate, George is talking again, what? what

was that George? I didn't hear ya, ay?

Club Tropicana,

Oh, you're saying Club Tropicana, me and

Khadijah,

Yeah, celebrate,

Well we'll have to do something mate,

You've worked hard, you deserve to unwind,

With the exam out the way, it'll be a weight off

your mind,

Sorry Khadijah, George is interrupting again,

George, what is it? What are you saying?

Yes, yes, I know George, I know, I tell her all the

time she is amazing,

Khadijah, I'm always praising,

She should be proud of herself,

She's done so well,

I agree, to cope with everything that life has

thrown at her,

To keep getting up after life has kicked her, to get

up stronger,

To come back even better,

She's got such a strong character,

Of her I couldn't be prouder,

She's a fighter,

A true inspiration, I wish I could be like her,

Will you bloody stop it now George with your

reference to another song,

This poem is already bloody long,

Khadijah might not bloody read it,

She might think look at the length of this, F that

s$#t,

Yes when she qualifies she will be able to have

everything she wants, all the nice things in life she

deserves,

Reward for what all her hard work earns,

What's that George? You're going?

Okay, good, now it's just me and you matey, let's

see if I can save this poem from complete ruin,

Yes, George though in this poem he's been

annoying,

With his interfering and interrupting,

Our friend George,

Did speak many a wise word,

You know I believe in you,

You should too,

In our friend George's words, you gotta have

faith,

You've got this, you can do this, you will do this,

the exam, okay.

Biscuits, Cookies and Other Goodies

No. 10

Khadijah, just another poem wishing you good luck in your exam. Not that you need it, you're brilliant and amazing but I've told you that a million times before. You're so clever, I believe in you buddy and I'm here for you always matey.

Unfortunately, I can't help you with any answers, you know I'm a dummy, I couldn't do what you're doing, I admire you matey. You've worked so hard for this and you're nearly there now matey, one big last push and I'll be here to cheer you over that finishing line.

As I said I'm no use whatsoever when it comes to helping you with your exam, you know if I could, I would so I'm afraid the best I can do to help matey is just keep giving you encouragement and support telling you that you can do this and will do this, I believe in you and so does our friend George and our little "Twix".

Oh and I try and help by keeping your energy levels up with Jaffa Cakes, Biscuits, Cookies, anything you fancy really and that you think will help, hence what inspired this poem, though we do have our treats regardless anyways don't we on a daily basis. Lol and not that we have to but we can justify ourselves by saying we're doing it because of your exam and some reading this will say why, but Mark, why do you have to eat them and keep your energy levels up you're not doing the exam and to them I say no, no I'm not but in solidarity with my matey. Hopefully the biscuits etc., they help to keep your energy levels up and help you get through your study and revision.

Anyway matey, wishing you all the best in the exam, you'll smash it because you're amazing and brilliant, you've got this buddy. xx

Of trying to help, I guess it was just my way,

As you will recall, when I would say,

Buddy, you got this,

As in I brought, a packet of biscuits,

Into your office,

Sometimes cookies,

But always some sort of goodies,

A particular favourite, Jaffa Cakes,

Guaranteed, always did bring a smile to your face,

As I said in your exam. You'll be ace!

This exam you're going to smash,

You're going to pass,

Biscuits, Cookies,

Or other goodies,

In hand, I'd always apologise to you and say,

unfortunately,

This is the best help I can be,

I'm a dummy,

I don't know any answers in your exam but I can

at least help keep you stocked with energy,

With Jaffa Cakes, biscuits, cookies and other

goodies,

To help get you through your studies,

You know that you, I'll be rooting for,

You're going to do brilliant and amazing, I'm

sure!

So if by keeping your energy levels up, I play a

small part,

Well then, that just makes me feel warm and glad

in my heart,

Good luck Khadijah,

I've got faith in ya, I'm right behind ya!

Where to Miss? To Celebrate

No. 11

Khadijah, not long now, the finish line is in sight, all your hard work will soon be rewarded. When your exam is over, I'll take you out to celebrate you being free from all that studying, my treat mate to say well done on all your hard work and try and help you de-stress. You put everyone else first, so let someone put you first and treat you after all the grueling studying and exam, let you unwind, relax and de-stress. You deserve it matey. Oh, and P.s, I'm super proud of you, it's not been easy for you but you've got there matey. Well done.

I promise,

After all this,

Your exam business,

By way of celebration at their finish,

And to de-stress,

I'll take you out to celebrate, anywhere you wish,

Just name the place Miss,

A treat after all your hard work,

A break, a chance to de-stress, it's well deserved,

My treat, on me,

Now from the exam stress and study, you're free,

Free from exam worry,

At least temporarily,

Until you get your results early in the new year,

When we can celebrate your pass with a cheer,

As you know, I believe in you,

And in the words of our friend George, you gotta

have faith, so believe in yourself too!

So after your exam we'll celebrate,

Just name the place mate,

Anywhere,

And I'll take you there!

Reminds me of Jack and Rose,

Everyone knows,

You know that scene,

You know the one I mean,

The one in the car, where he asks Rose, where to

Miss?

And he'll take her to wherever Rose does wish,

Rose says to the stars, and if that's where you said

you wanted to go,

I don't know how but, but I'd find a way of

getting you there you know?

So once your exam is over, we'll go and celebrate,

Anywhere you wish mate,

Just name the destination,

And I'll make it happen!

I'm proud of you, and you should be too.

A Guardian Angel – I Met You For A Reason

No. 12

Khadijah, I've told you the story behind this poem a million times, and you probably don't believe its true and I would never have had, had I never came across that YouTube video.

I'll cut some of the points out as they are in the poem and go straight to the main one, the reason behind this poem.

You remember me telling you about the YouTube video I watched about 10 signs you know your loved one has made it to the other side and are watching over you and that one sign, the main one the poem is about, is when they said, you won't know who or why, but they'll send someone into your life to sort of watch over you, someone you connect with and you'll know who when you meet them, it will stand out, and I told you that I strongly believe that person is you.

I've told you the reasons why I think this, obviously as you know, I don't have any family left but the way instantly, as soon as I met you, I don't know why because I find it really hard to open up to people and talk to people especially, feelings, emotions and personal stuff etc. but not with you I didn't, there was no hesitation, I just felt so at ease with you, like I could and can talk to you about anything, absolutely anything, tell you things, I've never told people before, even people I've known for years, clearly there is something so special about you and after watching that video, I believe whatever the reason, you were somehow chosen by God, Mum, Dad, I know it sounds crazy, I know and I would never have believed had I not watched that video.

Also how we've had shared and similar experiences is uncanny as if like some sort of destiny, fate thing to meet to be friends that confide in and support each other and be there for one another to somehow help each other through our experiences, I know, I'm not really explaining it well, I know, it's hard to explain this as it seems so unexplainable that yeah, well, no, I can't really explain, it's just, well you know, no, no I can't put it into words, best I move on, on this point. Lol

How you always check on me, back to the looking out for me again aren't we?, like a sort of Guardian Angel, checking I'm ok and how you just know when I'm not without me saying anything, you just uncannily know, you know me better than me, how you check if I've eaten and how you tell me to grab something to eat, rest and sleep well, get home safely, all that sometimes reminds me of something Mum and Dad would say to me.

You're an amazing person Khadijah, the most amazing I've ever met, the biggest, kindest heart, the most selfless person I've ever met, I honestly cannot believe how lucky I am to have met you and have a friend like you who looks out for me like you do, who always takes her precious time and wastes it on a fool like me knowing she will never ever be able to get that time back for something else.

And you know matey, it works both ways, I am always, always here for you anytime. You know I think the world of you buddy, I've told modest you how you've got me through stuff I would never have gotten through despite you saying you haven't done anything, you have matey, more than you'll ever know, just listening, or your pearls of wisdom, helping me see things clearly and with perspective or just making me smile everyday by just seeing you, or seeing one of them beautiful bright infectious smiles, making me laugh, just spending time with you makes me happy, our chats about anything, just you, just you buddy being you.

Well you're just amazing, I can't really say much else, well I could but you probably want to get to the end of the book before the next millennium. Lol.

But here it comes anyway, another massive thank you but I suppose the book is called Khadijah, a Thank you to ya!

Thank you.

Into my life you have come,

I believe sent by my Dad and Mum,

The chosen one,

Sent with love,

I believe with divine intervention from above,

From Heaven, have you fell?

Because you're like a Guardian Angel!

More than once, I'm sure,

That I've told you the story before,

You're probably sceptical,

And think I'm talking nonsensical,

I know what you mean,

I wouldn't have believed either, if that YouTube

video, I had not seen,

The video was 10 signs you know your loved

ones have made it to the other side and watching

over you,

As it mentioned some of the things that they do,

I recall I told you about a few,

Like if you have pets, they might start to behave

strangely,

As if they can sense a spirit or an entity,

Which is ghostly,

I've seen this with Winnie,

When he's just stood with his tail in the air,

There is nothing there,

But he just stops there and does stare,

You cannot break his gaze,

Him, you can't unfaze,

Even if you wave your hand in front of his eyes

to try to,

He just moves his head around you,

And continues staring,

Obviously there is something that he is sensing,

Another sign,

Was when they would interfere with time,

Clocks would stop or begin to chime,

Another sign might be,

Interfering with technology,

Interrupting the signals,

When it comes to electricals,

Playing havoc with TV's and aerials,

Or when they move stuff,

As you question and say that's not where, there,

that, I did put,

And so you put it back again,

Only to notice it has been moved again, leaving

you to ask, am I going insane?

But none of those reasons is what this poem is

about,

You'll probably think it's rubbish or coincidence

but I believe this without any shadow of a doubt,

In that YouTube video,

It says who, or why, at first you won't know,

But someone will be sent into your life, like a sort

of Guardian Angel,

Chosen by them to make sure you're okay and

well,

Why they choose that person, in time you'll tell,

You may not think and probably don't think it's
true,
But I believe it's you,
Just the way I feel so comfortable with you and
find you so easy to talk to,
How I can talk to you about anything,
How I feel I can open up to you about
everything,
Me,
I just felt it instantly,
A connection, a click, because of similar and
shared experiences we just fitted,
Like a couple of jigsaw pieces,
How I can be like an open book with you,
And the other little things that you do,
Like checking on me,
Have I had breakfast?, dinner? and Tea?,
To text you when I get home safely,
Just little things like that,
I know, I probably sound like a twat,
But things like that remind me of something

Mum and Dad would do,

Looking out for me through you,

It's just …

Just you, I just feel like you, I can trust,

Trust with anything, sharing my feelings,

emotions, personal stuff, hell I'd trust you even

with my life,

The times you've helped me through trouble and

strife,

How you've always given me good advice,

How since you came into my life you've always

been there,

You've showed me how you do care,

The nightly texts wishing each other good night

and to have sweet dreams,

Oh how much those texts means,

You've been there through times good and bad,

Times happy and sad,

You know how you always make me smile,

You always make me feel worthwhile,

You always make me happy,

Just by being in your company,

You give me a sense of importance,

You give me boosts in confidence,

You always find time for me,

Even though you're so busy,

And that time, you sacrificed on me when there is

much more important things than me, you'll

never recover,

The Lord, Mum, Dad have sure blessed me with

someone special like you Khadijah,

To send someone into my life, they couldn't have

found anyone better,

And though sadly, I know it won't last forever,

You, I'll forget never,

But can truly be thankful that once I was so

blessed,

As to have an amazing woman like you in my life,

Khadijah, you're truly the best.

So you, may God forever bless,

God, bless this real life Angel with nothing but

eternal happiness.

She's Alright Mama ... You'd Like her!

No. 13

Khadijah, a couple of things inspired this poem. I mean you know me well by now, how I often relate song lyrics or movie quotes into our conversations whatever subject we are talking about, serious or otherwise. You'll see elsewhere in this book what I mean about song lyrics and quotes in one of the other poems about that. Lol

I was recently listening to an Elvis Presley CD and the song "That's Alright Mama" played and it got me thinking, and I know I've told you before that when I've been to Mum's grave, I've told her about you, how amazing you are and how you've really looked out for me, always checking on me, checking I've eaten something, checking I've got home safely, how I just feel so comfortable with you and can talk to you about anything and be like an open book, something I struggle with, talking, but not with you, instantly, as soon as I met you, I just felt so at ease and comfortable, the list goes on, you get the drift, well you know what you do even though you're dismissive and don't believe you've done anything. I've told you before it's like you're a guardian angel and perhaps its Mum that had a word with the man upstairs and sent you into my life, for, of course, I'm forever grateful. I'd told you about that YouTube video I'd watched which I won't go into again because I've already mentioned it in the book in another poem and the background of that but again you know anyway.

You know, I know it sounds daft, but every night I always ask my Mum to look after you and watch over you like a guardian angel, you know keep you safe and this Elvis song when listening to it, made me think how I know, looking down from above, Mum would like you, she'd think you're alright and Mama, she is, Khadijah, is alright, she's a good'un, she's the loveliest, sweetest human I've ever met, she has the biggest heart and is the most selfless person I've ever met, always putting others first, she's an amazing human, I'm blessed and so damn lucky to be able to call her a friend. So Mama, she's alright Mama, you'd like her!

Mum,

Though you're gone,

I know you still look on,

She's alright mama,

I know you'd like her,

Khadijah,

A girl like no other,

Every night I always ask ya,

To look and watch over her,

To be her guardian angel,

Because she's so bloody special,

So kind and gentle,

She's funny and bubbly,

She's sweet and she's lovely,

She's beautiful inside and out,

When I come to visit your grave, she's the one

I've told you about,

She's selfless,

A big heart, pure and full of goodness,

She's always thinking of others,

Always putting everyone else first,

A quality that's one of her best but also her worst,

Because who's there for her when she needs them

and feeling hurt?

I hope she knows that if she needs someone, for

her, to be there,

Then I'm here for her, anytime, anywhere,

Like for me. she has been,

For example, I'll tell you what I mean,

Like how she always knew,

When I was feeling blue,

How she always knew what to do,

To make me smile again,

To get me back on my game,

To help see things with perspective and clearly,

And that things are not ever that bad really,

Or like how just being in her company,

Makes me feel all warm and fuzzy,

I just feel so happy,

Or like how in this world of mine,

She makes me feel like I'm basking in permanent

sunshine,

How I can talk to her so openly and freely,

It's crazy,

With her, I'm just like an open book, talking to

her comes easy,

Talking feelings and stuff,

I always found tough,

But not with Khadijah, I just feel so at ease and

comfortable,

It just flows oh so natural,

Clearly she's very special,

Maybe it has something to do with you?

Did you have a word with the man upstairs? It

sounds like something you'd do?

Did you ask him to send me a Guardian Angel?

And they sent someone into my life truly special?

Khadijah, so amazing that surely from heaven she

must have fell!

It's just funny however since I first met her,

That it seems that I'd known her forever,

She's a true Godsend,

And everyday I count my blessings for being sent

such an amazing friend,

So, Mum, I conclude,

That of her, you'd approve,

Khadijah,

She's alright mama,

You'd like her.

Open Book

No. 14

Khadijah, I've told you this a million times too, and I don't know why but with you, I feel like I can be an open book, I just feel so comfortable with you, I feel that I can tell you anything, tell you everything, it's a massive, massive thing for me, because as you know, I build walls up and bottle stuff up but with you it's the opposite, you knock them walls down and I trust you completely, it's a feeling I got instantly when I met you, it's strange, you have to be pretty damn special to make me feel like that, well no have to about it, you are, you are special, you're a special person matey.

Now I've told you my theory on it, that YouTube video I watched and it said your departed ones as a way of looking out for you and telling you they're ok on the other side will send someone into your life who is like a guardian angel type figure, they look out for you, etc. you'll know who when they enter, you'll just know and I've told you I believe its you just purely how someone like me who finds it hard to talk feelings, emotions that deep stuff, etc. only just meets you and yet can be so open, like an open book and feel so comfortable with you that he feels he can tell you anything, tell you everything, that's huge, that's really huge for me. So thank you buddy.

From the moment I first met you, I just felt so comfortable with you. You are a true diamond Khadijah, a big heart full of gold, you're the most caring, kind, sweetest, most selfless person I've ever met. I'm so blessed to have a friend like you.

Pretty much instantly,

I felt with you I could talk openly and freely,

I don't know why Khadijah,

Must have been your aura,

I've always found it tough,

Talking about personal stuff,

Always bottled that s#£t up,

But with you I'm just like an open book,

Opening the pages and revealing all,

With you, out my heart, I can pour,

Like a tell all biography,

I trust you completely,

Nothing is off limits,

Feelings, emotions, secrets,

With you, I feel comfortable telling them all,

Somehow you've knocked down that long
standing wall,

That around my heart, around myself I had
erected,

I guess to feel protected,

As until meeting you, there was no-one I really
trusted,

You, I can tell you anything,

I can talk to you about everything,

My inner most thoughts,

My feelings when I'm out of sorts,

My emotions, my every feeling,

With you I'm so comfortable with them revealing,

Some of the stuff I tell you, anyone else I
wouldn't dare,

But with you I feel so comfortable that with you,
that stuff, I feel I can share,

Wholeheartedly,

I trust you completely,

Something that isn't easy for me,

I know whatever I share with you is in the
strictest confidence,
Staying just between us,
Which matters most when I find it so hard to
trust,
You must be pretty damn special,
Because with you I just feel so comfortable,
With you, I'm an open book.

It Was Like We Had Known
Each Other Forever

No. 15

Khadijah, I've told you this before, but with you I just feel like I've known you forever and that's a truly special feeling.

I recall how I told you that pretty much instantly, I felt a connection with you, a click, I don't know what it is, your aura perhaps, truth is I don't know but I know whatever it is, whatever the reason, I just felt so comfortable and at ease with you and that I could and can be like an open book with you. That is testament to you my friend for making me feel like that. I can tell you anything, my deepest and most personal things and I just feel so comfortable, which if you ask anyone I don't just open up to anyone, I usually find talking feelings and emotions hard but not with you, you're clearly a very special person Khadijah, hell you've even seen me cry! (ssshhh don't tell anyone!) Oh they'll read it here – oh never mind!

Yeah, I just felt/feel like I've known you forever. I wish it was forever, I wish I had known you longer matey. In truth I could know you for eternity and I'd still wish it was longer that's how highly I regard you buddy.

I also recall when I had been a bit distant, and not my usual self, I hadn't chatted with you or really seen you, you noticed, you messaged me, asking if I was ok? Was I hiding from you again? You ordered ne to pop to your office lunch time. I'll admit, I felt like a naughty schoolboy being summoned to the Headmistress and thought, I'm in trouble here, she is going to shout at me but of course you didn't, you just told me to sit down and talk to you, I tried to say I don't want to bother you matey, you have your own stuff going on without this idiot taking up your valuable time but of course you insisted and listened and were amazing as always you have that gift of always making me smile, making me think more clearly, making me see things ain't as bad as I think and always give me a different way of thinking and help me think more clearly and with perspective. You touched my heart when you told me you're always there, you're always here for me and matey, that's both ways, please know, always, that I am here for you too. Yeah, you always do somehow know or can tell when with me, all is not well. I don't know how you do it, but you do, you clearly know me so well, probably know me better than me! Lol. Perhaps it's like we've known each other forever.

Going back to how it feels like I've known you forever, how I just instantly felt so comfortable with you and that I could be an open book with you, tell you anything etc. You may or may not recall when I told you about that YouTube video I'd watched about how you know that a departed loved one has made it to the other side but are still looking out for you and letting you know they're ok etc. and there was signs like if you have a pet, they might act strangely as if they can sense or see a spirit, things might unexplainably move from where you have put it, you move it back and it moves again, clocks and electricals get interfered with you know that sort of thing but the most interesting one which is the one I told you about and you may think it's a load of rubbish but I'm not so sure, but it said they would send someone into your life and you won't know why or for what purposes but you'll just feel a connection, it's like they have sent someone to sort of look out for you, like a guardian angel that sort of thing, and that's what I feel with you, about you, the fact that I can just talk to you about anything and everything and feel so comfortable and be so open, like I said you've got to be pretty damn special for me to feel like that because I really struggle to talk feelings, emotions, personal stuff with anyone but for some reason with you I didn't feel any of that, I just felt and do feel I can talk to you about anything and did so from the moment I first met you. Like I said it's testament to you. You're amazing and clearly a truly special human the likes of which I'll never ever meet someone as amazing as you again.

So I guess all that's left to say again is another thank you.

I know this is Rose's line but I trust you.

It was like you I had always knew,

When I first met you,

It didn't take us long to get to know each other,

The chats, the laughs that we shared in those

special times spent together,

It was like I had known you forever,

When I was feeling down and low,

Somehow you would just know,

Know how to make me feel better,

It was like I had known you forever,

With you I just felt comfortable and at ease

instantly,

I felt I could talk to you about anything openly

and freely,

I still remember the time I opened up to you

about my depression and feeling under pressure,

You didn't judge, you were kind and sweet and

said I could talk to you whenever,

It was like I had known you forever,

Always will I remember,

The memories, the moments, the times spent

together,

Forever those moments and memories I will

treasure,

It was like I had known you forever.

You Know Me So Well

No. 16

Khadijah, a poem I've knocked up about how you just seem to know me so well, you probably know me better than I know me.

I don't know how you do it, but you just seem to know when I'm not myself, I can't hide anything from you, you just know.

I remember that text you sent me, "Hiding from me again" and then another saying "Pop up dinner time", you'll probably laugh now, I probably told you anyway but anyway I remember reading that and thinking oh shit, I'm in the shit now, I felt like a naughty kid being summoned to the headmistress. I remember walking in and you telling me to sit down and we had a chat, talked it through, and you're amazing and brilliant but you know that, I tell you all the time what I think of you, I've told you before I think the world of you matey, you're amazing, but you always have a way of making me feel better, you always know what to say and how to word things, you always help me see things with perspective and clarity, to see things clearly, to see things from a different way.

I've told you countless times before you never fail to make me smile, you always do, you're

always that sunshine on the darkest of days.
You're gifted, you always make me feel lifted
you're just amazing.

Though we haven't known each other for long,

You just know when something is wrong,

I don't know how, but you can just tell,

When with me, all is not well!

You can tell if I'm not okay,

You can tell if I'm having an off day,

But to cheer me up you can always find a way,

You're gifted,

Because whenever I'm with you I feel lifted,

You always make me smile,

To make sure I'm ok you always go that extra

mile,

You see me with a frown,

You know how to turn that upside down,

As even when you are so busy,

You go out your way to make time for me,

When you text me to summon me to your office,

I think Uh-oh, I'm in the s##t!

It's like being summoned to the headmistress,

As you tell me off for staying hid,

You tell me to sit down will ya!

Come tell Auntie Khadijah,

I told you before, you're like the sister,

The sister I never had,

And like a sister, you just know when I'm sad,

And so then I take a seat and we have a chat,

And you always give me good advice and that,

You always help me to see things with

perspective and clearly,

Providing me with a moment of clarity,

You help me see that things are never that bad

really,

You have your own stuff to worry about and for

bothering you I feel guilty,

Though you, me, you always reassure,

As you say you don't mind, it's what friends are

for,

It's what friends do,

I am here for you,

You're always there to talk to,

For that I'm eternally grateful,

You're so bloody special,

And that's vice-versa,

Because I'm here for you too, Khadijah,

Should you ever need,

My shoulder is here to cry on and lean,

Friends, there for each other,

For each other, nothing is too much bother,

For each other, we look out,

It's what being friends is all about,

But even so,

I still find it amazing though,

How you just know,

When all is not well, how you can tell,

But I guess you just know me so well,

So thank you,

Thank you to you, the most beautiful, amazing,

kind hearted, sweetest person I've ever knew.

I Trust You

No. 17

Khadijah, another Jack and Rose reference (there's been a few in this book hasn't there).

I trust you, a line Jack said to Rose when he was handcuffed and Rose had to chop the cuffs with the axe and he trusted her not to cut his hand off and this is like our Jack and Rose thingy majig, I trust you.

Khadijah, I trust you. I trust you completely. It's usually hard for me to trust people like I trust you, it takes a long time but not with you, you were different, you're clearly very special, I've told you that and I've told you this before, but ever since I met you, I've felt just so at ease with you, so comfortable with you, like an open book, nothing is hidden from you, I feel I can tell you anything and everything, I feel like I've known you forever, I wish I had known you longer, you know, even if I had known you forever, I'd still wish I'd known you for longer!

I've touched on that YouTube video a couple of times in this book, but I believe for whatever reason you were sent in to my life and I'm blessed and so lucky for that happening, you're like a guardian angel and you know I think the absolute world of you buddy and trust you completely.

Thank you, Thank you Khadijah for being the most amazing, sweetest, kindest, most selfless person I've ever met, you're a special human you know that buddy, thank you for coming into my life, brightening up my world, being amazing and just being there, there to talk to, to confide in, share my feelings, emotions, secrets, inner most thoughts with, for making me feel that comfortable with you that I can be like an open book with you. Thank you.

I trust you Rose. I trust you Khadijah.

I trust you,

I'd like to think that you trust me too,

I trust you, a line from Titanic, a film everyone

knows,

I trust you, a line Jack said to Rose,

I trust you, a line I've said to you, Khadijah,

I trust you, a feeling I had from the very first

moment I met ya!

I trust you, like you, forever I have knew,

I trust you, I really, really do,

I trust you with anything,

I trust you with everything,

I trust you to talk to when I'm out of sorts,
I trust you with my secrets and inner
most thoughts,
I trust you in times of trouble and strife,
I'd trust you with my life!
I trust you wholeheartedly and completely,
I trust you, it shows how special you are to me,
I trust you, Khadijah, I trust you, buddy!

Jack and Rose

No. 18

Khadijah, how could I not do a poem or include a poem about our special Jack and Rose thing huh, buddy?

You know this is our special thing. How it makes me smile and hopefully you too, when we get our little notes off each other and we sign them off Jack and Rose.

I recall when we said we're like Jack and Rose, Jack has your back, you jump, I jump remember, we're a team and I'm always here for you no matter what.

I remember when we'd meet at home time at the bottom of the grand staircase (I know, our staircase is more bland than grand but work with me here buddy, lol) I'd be at the bottom of the stairs feeling like Jack, waiting for you, (Rose) to come into view, always reminded me of Rose, you're always dressed so elegantly like a proper lady like Rose in the movie, and coming down the stairs you would have seen me smile as you'd say oh you waited for me, sounding surprised as I'd say I don't mind and then we'd leave the office together and say our goodbyes on the car park and it was a joke between us on a daily basis as I'd say just a little before 5p.m when I'd text you to say meet you at the usual time at the bottom of the grand staircase?, and you'd say yes please.

That's what I mean about our fantastic, quirky bond and friendship, only we get it, no-one else would get it, it's our special thing that sort of makes our friendship fun and special, I love it.

But perhaps the biggest thing Khadijah, is how I just totally and completely trust you, like Jack did with Rose when Rose had to chop the handcuffs off in the film, and he says I trust you Rose, you can do it. Mate, If I was handcuffed, I'd trust you to do that too! Lol. But yeah, honestly, Khadijah, I trust you like I trust no other, I'd trust you with my life, I trust you with my inner most thoughts, I tell you things I tell no-one else, I just feel so comfortable and at ease with you, I can't explain why, but ever since I met you I just felt like I could tell you anything, stuff I've never ever been able to tell anyone or talk to about, feelings, emotions, personal stuff, obviously you're just special, you gotta be to make me feel like that, because that sort of stuff I struggle with yet with you I don't know, I just feel so relaxed, so comfortable, like I can be an open book, like I can open my heart and pour everything out, I've never been able to do that, and I don't know why, but I just feel different with you, I completely trust you. For that, I can only say thank you.

Jack and Rose,

Their story everyone knows,

Jack and Rose, from that movie classic,

Jack and Rose from Titanic.

We have our own special version of that

friendship,

Like Jack,

I've always got your back,

We have a special friendship, always looking out

for one another,

You jump, I jump remember,

We have a bond,

A friendship that is strong,

You know Jack will do anything for you Rose,

You know how that saying goes,

Jack,

He's got your back!

You know it's what I always say to you,

When for you, something for you I do,

Whenever you ask me to,

You say aww you're so kind,

As I say honestly, I don't mind,

Anything I can do to help and make things easier,

Anything to take some of the stress and pressure,

Anything for ya,

Khadijah,

Jack and Rose remember,

Always looking out for each other,

Nothing for me is too much bother,

As long as you are okay,

That's Jack's way,

Me and you, we're a team buddy,

You can rely on me,

The fun and quirkiness in our unique special

friendship shows,

When we sign off emails and messages between

us signed Jack and Rose,

Or a little sticky post it note,

Signed Jack or Rose, after the little message we've

wrote,

Other things in our friendship remind me of Jack

and Rose,

You must remember the grand staircase scene,

It's a scene everyone knows,

How it reminds me of you and I, I'll explain what

I mean,

Remember when I used to wait for you at the

bottom of the staircase at home time patiently,

I've told you this before too, how you remind of

Rose, always dressed so elegantly,

A proper lady,

So, for you, I'd be waiting at the bottom of the

staircase,

When you'd come into view, a smile would be on

my face,

As together we'd leave the place,

As we'd say our goodbyes on the carpark, I'd say

see you tomorrow at the same time at the bottom

of the grand staircase,

I know, our staircase is more bland,

Than grand,

But you'd say yes,

As before we'd go our separate ways for home,

I'd say later on I'll send our usual goodnight text,

And then,

Tomorrow we'd do it all again,

A routine I always looked forward too,

At the bottom of the staircase, greeting you,

It is funny,

Because now I can't help but think of you and

me,

When I watch this movie,

Whenever it comes on TV,

I just smile and think of thee,

And do you know the biggest thing that reminds

me,

It's where Jack says Rose, I trust you,

And Khadijah, I trust you, I really do,

You jump, I jump remember,

Jack and Rose forever,

Jack,

He's always got your back!

KHADIJAH, JACK & ROSE - REMEMBER.

KHADIJAH, IV'E ALWAYS GOT YOUR
BACK BUDDY.

I'll Be There For You

No. 19

Khadijah, you know by now or should know, but I'm always here for you buddy, always! Jack and Rose remember!

I'll be there for you anytime, any place if you ever need me.

I'll be there for you to celebrate every success, looking on proudly and saying well done matey.

I'll be there for you to always encourage and support you in all your dreams, goals and ambitions and say YES YOU CAN! You're Khadijah, you're a star, you're amazing, you CAN do it, you WILL do it!

I'll be there for you if you ever fall to catch you and put you back on your feet and say come on buddy, I've got you, Jack has your back Rose, let's go again, I'm right behind you, beside you, wherever you want me or need me but I'm supporting you, cheering you on, I'm your biggest fan encouraging you.

Sticking with Jack and Rose, mate, you know I'm always, always here for you, I'll be that wardrobe door for you to lean on if you ever need to cling to someone for support, someone to talk to, lean on, hit (as long as you're gentle with me) lol! Vent at, anything, you know I'm here for you for anything buddy. I promise, I'll never let you down. I'll never fail you when you need me.

If you're ever that person that feels like you're drowning, I'll be the one that reaches out a hand for you to grab, I promise. If you're ever the one that feels they are in a crowded room screaming at the top of your voice and no-one is hearing you, I'm all ears buddy, I hear you, I'm there buddy, I'm there for you, buddy.

I care, I'm there, just like for me, you have always been there ever since we met.

P.S I Just realised we have another song, "I'll be there for you", pretty sure it was the theme tune from Friends. Not sure if you ever watched it or not but anyway for you, if you ever need me, you know I'm here for you, right? Buddy.

Hopefully by now you know me well enough,

Hopefully by now you know I'll be here for you

when times are tough,

When you're sailing the seas of life and the waters

are a little rough,

When you're the Captain of your ship and feeling

alone,

Anytime, anyplace, just pick up the phone,

And I'll be your first mate!

Never hesitate,

There I'll be,

If you ever need me,

I'll be there,

I care,

For another Jack and Rose reference, prepare,

If ever you feel overwhelmed, lost, alone, don't

know where to turn, drowning or unsure,

Then matey, I'll be your wardrobe door,

Cling on to me for support, it's what friends are

for,

Rest assured,

You, I will always be there for,

Night or day,

You know I'll help in any way,

If you ever just need someone to listen, or hit, or

vent at,

I'll be, and do all that, For you I'll be there, for

you, for that!

If you ever need me to help you out with your

work load and take some of the pressure and

stress off you,

Give it to me and tell me what to do,

And consider it done as you say,

For you, I'll always be there come what may,

Anytime, anyplace, I'd get there someway,

Yep,

I'll be there for you always, by your side, on your

side, behind you, every single step,

Should you ever need me anytime or anywhere,

For you, I'll always be there,

Every dream, every nightmare,

For you, I'll always be there,

Supporting you,

All the way through,

It's what friends do,

Like our Rose and Jack,

I've always got your back!

Through thick and thin, good times and bad,

Whether you're happy or whether you're sad,

I'll be there for you,

It's what friends do,

I'll be there for you when you're down,

I'll try and put that beautiful, bright smile back on

your face,

I'll be there for you to make you smile and laugh

like I'm your own personal clown,

I'll try and fill your day with fun and laughter until

we're falling all over the place,

I'll be there for you, no matter how many times

you fall,

I'll be there for you always, to pick you up once

more,

Again and again,

The result will aways be the same,

Time after time,

I'll be there for you always, Khadijah, this special,

amazing friend of mine,

When you're standing proud and tall,

Celebrating your accomplishments and successes,

I'll be there for you, through them all,

Patting you on the back,

Saying well done from Jack,

I'm proud of you,

It's what friends do,

I'll be there for you through it all,

I'll be there for you always, so if you need me,

just call,

I do,

And I always will believe in you,

Forget Rachel, Phoebe and Monica,

Ross, Joey and Chandler,

They ain't got what we got, - Mark and Khadijah,

We're like Jack and Rose, remember!

I know it's supposed to be your line, but I won't

let go,

If you need a helping hand, If you need me, you

know,

I'll always be there for you,

It's just what friends do!

On your side until the end,

Forever your friend,

Yours truly,

Mark. Your buddy. xx

I'd Go To Battle For You …

No. 20

Khadijah, just a quick poem to reiterate what you already (or should know) and that's I'm always on your side, you know I'm your biggest fan and that I believe in you and I know unfortunately I can't help you with your exam, I'm a dummy, I'd be no use at all but you know if I could, I would, I can be your cheerleader though (I'm not wearing the skirt though, not with my legs. Lol) and give you encouragement and tell you, you're going to do great, and you will, you're so clever and knowing you only a short time, I know how hard you have worked and how amazing you are, you haven't had things easy, all the things life has thrown at you and that's just in the short time I've known you, but you no matter how many times you've been knocked down you get back up, you're an inspiration to me on how you keep doing it. I believe in you matey, in the words of our friend George, "gotta have faith". You will pass mate, you're brilliant and I'm always behind you, anything I can do to take some of the stress off you ahead of your exam you know I'd do it. Sadly the only help I've been able to give really is keeping you supplied with energy, jaffa cakes, hobnobs, different teas etc but be assured mate, I'm right behind you and believe in you. I'm always on your side mate. Jack and Rose remember.

Can you believe at the end of the poem I literally just compared myself to a dog, a bloody dog! Lol.

Whatever you do,

You know I'm always right behind ya, supporting

you,

You know with you I'll stand shoulder to

shoulder,

You know I'll be your loyal soldier,

You know I'm with you through every Battle,

You know I'll be there to pick you up anytime

you fell,

Through thick and thin, rain or shine,

I'm always here for you, my beautiful, amazing,

special friend of mine,

You know for you I'd go to war,

You know for you I'd do anything for,

For you I'd walk through hell, fire and brimstone,

Here for you always matey, I promise you'll never

have to face anything alone,

Anything I can do to, you, assist,

I'm always at your service Miss,

I've always got your back,

You know that,

Rose, remember, I'm your Jack,

Like man's best friend,

I'm forever on your side until the end.

You Make The Sun Shine Everyday

No. 21

Khadijah, I had to put this poem in here, I told you before how, and I don't how or why, but around you, I just feel so happy all the time, you're sunshine, you brighten up my day, my life, it could be pissing down with rain, it could be dark, it could be gloomy, but nah, not in my world, not when you're around, I'm basking in permanent sunshine so just wrote this to thank you for brightening up my life and being the reason I smile everyday when you're around. Hey In fact, I think I've just solved the NHS problem, they could prescribe you as you always make me feel better when I'm feeling low.

Outside it was raining,

As we were in your office talking, eh, more

complaining,

Health being the topic of conversation,

As we dissected the problem with the nation,

Discussing the extortionate cost,

Concluding the health system is bost,

Concluding its so expensive to be healthy,

Looking out the window you said look, it's always

106

rainy,

In this country we don't get enough vitamin D,

Not enough sunshine,

I smiled and said I don't have that problem in this

world of mine,

You smiled too,

As you must have remembered what a couple of

days earlier I had said to you,

As I said in my world you make the sun shine

everyday,

I don't know, but you just seem to have a way,

As when everything seems, gloomy and dark and

no chink of light,

You make my world bright,

In the dark, you're that light,

It could be raining all the time,

But in your presence I'm basking in glorious

sunshine,

My life is never grey,

When you're around as you make the sun shine

everyday,

Because in your company,

I just feel so damn happy,

You just brighten up my day,

You make my dark clouds go away,

You make the sun shine,

In this world of mine,

It's never dull and grey,

When you're about,

The sun is always out,

It's always shining in my world, you make the sun

shine everyday.

You're A Star!

Khadijah, just a poem about your star. Again, I'm sorry with how long it took to come with Royal Mail. Still, I hope it was worth the wait buddy.

You know you always make me smile and it made me smile when you said you loved it and was blown away by the gesture saying it was unique and above and beyond.

Well, I just wanted to do something special but different. You have heard me several times tell you what a star you are, and with your own star, you're literally a star forever burning and shining bright, the brightest of stars. The star just happens to be in your star sign constellation Scorpius (Scorpio) which I thought would be cool.

I wanted something that would last forever not just a couple of days like flowers or chocolates and this star will long out last you and I and you'll forever be remembered you will always exist and you will never ever just be a faded memory buddy. You'll live forever matey. I know I'll never ever forget you right up until I take my last breath. You're the most amazing person I've ever met, so selfless, kind, sweet, caring, I could go on and on and on praising you and I have told you enough times what I think of you, how I think the world of you buddy and hopefully this book does that justice and tells you/shows you.

I thought it would also be nice because if we ever drifted apart which I so hope we never do but if we did, even if we were millions of miles apart, if we both looked at your star it would somehow seem that we were still near that somehow we could still see each other, it probably sounds stupid I know, but yeah, to me, you wouldn't seem to far away. Or if we did drift apart then maybe, I hope that perhaps, that maybe, you may look at your star and perhaps somehow remember me. I know I'll always remember you and when the time comes for me to leave this world and God or his Angels ask me what about life did you enjoy or love most? I shall say easy, time spent in your company, as matey I cherish every second spent with you, I don't know how you do it but I just always feel happy with you, in your presence, and so I just want to say thanks again for every precious moment spent in your company and hope we have many, many more moments and memories yet to come matey.

I also remember saying to you, you could tell your nieces and nephews that Auntie Khadijah is always watching you now from the sky too so you have to be good boys and girls. I'd also comfortingly feel that you were looking over me too, looking out for me like you do, sort of protecting me.

I know I'll be wishing upon your star and if you do too, I hope all your wishes and dreams come true matey.

So matey keep shining bright like your star lighting up the world like you do mine by just simply being in it.

I always said you were a star,

Now you have your own, shining bright in a

galaxy afar,

Thought it'd be a nice touch if it was in your star

sign constellation,

Perhaps something you and I can look to for

inspiration,

Your nieces and nephews can look at it with

wonder and imagination,

Could even be used as discipline action,

To your nieces and nephews say, you see that

bright star shining,

That's me, Auntie Khadijah, so be good boys and

girls because I'm always watching,

It seemed so apt,

I don't know, you might think it's daft,

The choice seemed obvious,

The constellation Scorpius,

Scorpio being your star sign,

You know by now how it works, this mind of

mine,

For you, I just wanted to do something original,

Something truly special,

Something eternal,

Something different,

Something heartfelt and meant,

I wanted something better, something that would

stand out more than just chocolates and flowers,

Something that would last more than just a few

hours,

This will last for all eternity,

Will live long after you and me,

This star signifies that you'll never ever be a faded

memory,

You and me may be gone,

But in years to come,

With your star, you'll forever live on,

You, people will always remember,

You'll live forever,

Forever shining bright amongst the stars,

You'll be shooting across the skies on your star,

no need for cars,

You smiled and said this gift is unique, special,

above and beyond,

I said, yeah, well you know of you, I'm fond,

I just wanted to do something special,

For such a beautiful, amazing girl,

A thank you,

For all that you do,

I told you that if it wasn't for you,

These past few weeks, past few months, I would

never have made it through,

I said you're just like your star, shining bright,

Because in my life, you're that beautiful guiding

light,

And you smiled as I said you already light up my

days now with your star shining bright,

You'll light up my night,

In the midst of the dark twilight,

You may or may not recall,

That in your office,

Talking about this,

I got emotional,

As I said I just somehow thought that even if we

drift apart,

If we look to your star,

From each other we'll never seem too far,

We'll always seem close by,

You can now see why this made me cry,

Anyway, wherever I am and wherever you are,

Looking at your star,

We could be millions of miles apart but it

somehow wouldn't seem that far,

It'll be like we can still somehow see each other,

Like somehow we're still together,

Still connected no matter between us, the

distance,

But know that if you ever needed me, I'd be there
in an instance,
I told you I'd probably be looking at your star for
guidance,
I said we could wish on your star and hope they
all come true,
And Khadijah, for you,
I really hope they do,
I really hope you get all you dream and wish for,
All the happiness in the world and so much more,
That you find your lucky dream guy that you, he
will adore,
That he treats you with respect and that you, he
does worship,
He would truly be the world's luckiest guy and I
hope he'd realise it,
For Khadijah, you deserve all life's nice things,
You deserve nothing but good blessings,
I wish you nothing but the best,
And as I say goodnight looking at your star I say
night, night Khadijah and God bless,

Khadijah, continue to burn bright,

You'll forever and always be my shining light,

Illuminating my life matey,

And so, if we ever drift apart, I hope that your

star, whenever you do see,

That maybe, somehow, you might remember me,

Because Khadijah, I promise, I'll never ever

forget thee,

And with your star,

I'll take comfort that you're never too far!

No matter where you are.

5 Star

Khadijah, it's not just me who thinks you're amazing matey, but the client's too, well done on your five star ratings, I've told you before how great you are and now from google you can see that's it's not just me that thinks that either. You should be very proud. You're doing amazing!

See, what did I tell ya,

Khadijah,

Not just me who thinks you're amazing,

Not just me who, you, is praising,

Just look at the great review after review,

At the firm you may be new,

But the client's clearly love you,

Just check out google!

You're gonna go far,

With your reviews of 5 star after 5 star,

Whether it's 5 stars, 10 out of 10, 100% percent,

whatever the scale,

Khadijah, you, we all hail,

You should be very proud you're doing great,

So well done mate,

I'm proud of you,

And you should be too,

You, I'm gonna keep praising,

Because you're bloody amazing,

You're a star,

And you're gonna go far!

Crazy

No. 24

Khadijah, this is one of the latest poems in the book added in late because the memory was only created a couple of weeks ago, it was Friday and we were in your office, you asked about any news on the book, I said yeah, was waiting on a delivery date but hoped it would be soon hopefully by next week, obviously since I added this poem in.

I told you I just wanted to do something special, a thank you for everything you've done for me, as usual, you being modest played it down, saying you hadn't done anything, I said you had, being there to talk to, for always making me smile everyday, all that. You smiled and joked and called me crazy (in an endearing, jokey, kind way) … (At least I hope you meant it that way!) lol. You said most people get someone a thank you card, not you, you write a whole book.

I said well you know me matey, I'm wired differently, I just wanted to do something different, something special, I said I hoped it didn't make you cry, laugh yes, but cry no, well not much any way, I admitted, I had shed a tear or several writing the book, because you're special, it brought back the memories of our magical moments together (to me they're

119

magical and cherished) I said hopefully some of them make you laugh, like the one about playing our games when we go for a walk into town and sit on our bench. Moments like that I treasure, I treasure every single second spent with you Khadijah, I'll never forget them.

You said and we'll have many more memories together. I felt a bit teary because I'd love that.

We did touch on your star as I said and yes this book further ensures you'll always be remembered as it will always be here like your star, you'll never be forgotten, I told you in that moment, I'll never forget you as I told you you're the most sweetest, most amazing, most special person I'd ever met and that I think the world of you, you've heard me tell you that a million times though, ok, not a million but not far off! I said future generations will be able to know how amazing you were/are long after we're gone.

I told you that I would push and push the book to sell it and sell lots of copies and that all the money made from it is yours and I hoped it would be able to work for you, I said I don't need the money, I wrote the book for you and anything from it monetary wise its yours, it's your book, its for you. You said I didn't have to do this, I said I want to. You said I was so kind and sweet and thoughtful, I said I just wanted to say thank you and that you were special and I told you how much you mean to me buddy and that I think the world of you.

You smiled and said you can't wait to see it. I said I just hoped you liked it as I want it to be special and perfect for you anything less won't do.

It was a Fridee,

When you called me crazy,

In a way that was endearing and jokey,

At least I hope so,

It was as we were having a convo,

As you asked about the book,

As I said look,

I Just wanted to do something different,

something special,

You said I was so kind and thoughtful,

I said I just wanted to do something to say thank

you,

For all that you do,

You being you, so modest and said you haven't

done anything,

I said you have, your listening and being there for

me, to me, it just means everything,

Without you,

I don't think I would have made it through,

You laughed and said most people would get a

thank you card to say thanks, but not me,

I wanted to do something special see,

Something unique and hopefully special,

Something that lasts eternal,

Something that will last long after you and I are

gone,

The book will ensure you will forever live on,

Future generations to come,

Will be able to read this and say she sure was a

special one,

Yep you'll never be forgotten,

This will help ensure people know you were, you

are a beautiful, special, amazing, one in a billion

woman,

You smiled and said thank you, as you said I

don't do things by halves,

As you then referred to your star,

I said and with the book I can write what I

couldn't fit in thank you cards,

You said bless you, you always go the extra mile,

Oh how I did smile,

Feeling all warm and fuzzy,

I said you know me,

I must be wired differently,

Or if and as you like, crazy,

You said it,

As you know, I often go with idiot,

I said when I get it, you'll have the very first copy,

I said I'll sign it from me,

I said you'll have to promise to sign mine,

You said you would no problem, fine,

I said I hoped to have it delivered next week,

A few weeks earlier you had a tiny sneak peak,

Of the sort of poems to expect,

This book, because its for you, I just want it to be

perfect,

Because you mean so much to me,

I said I hope it captures every (well to me anyway)

special memory,

Memories of our chats,

Our laughs,

Time spent together,

I hope we get to create and share many a more

memory and a many more chapter,

You smiled and said ah, bless you, of course we

will,

There's more to come still,

Memories, we'll have many more,

I smiled, I said, yeah, I'm sure,

Jack and Rose forevermore,

Right?

Right, you said smiling bright,

Yep, Jack and Rose you confirmed with that

beautiful smile, sweet and lovely,

And that was good enough confirmation for me,

I did get a little teary,

But thankfully, or at least I don't think you did,

you didn't see,

Or you probably would have thought what a

pathetic softy,

I admitted when writing some of the poems I got

emotional,

Because I thought of you and they're personal,

Because you're just so special,

I've told you often enough that you're bloody

wonderful,

A bloody marvel!

I said I hoped they made you laugh but hopefully

not cry,

To express my gratitude to you and capture every

treasured memory we've shared, I did try,

Hopefully this book does this,

That you love the book and that its perfect is my

only wish,

This book, I can't wait for you to see,

So come on, hurry up, bloody delivery!

You Crack Me Up

No. 25

Khadijah, just a short poem here.

You've probably never met anyone as daft as this idiot here I dare say. Khadijah, I love our friendship, how we make each smile and laugh, I love that I can crack you up with a crap joke (and lets admit some of them are pretty lame) or a funny story or saying something daft and crazy. I hope I can continue making you laugh, making you smile for a long, long time to come, I hope we have many more chapters to write together in this beautiful, wonderful, quirky friendship of ours and many, many more laughs together.

Thank you and thank you for being the reason I smile, I laugh, I look forward to work everyday (except when you're not there) lol. Then I'm a miserable sod lol.

Here's to more cracking you up (not that much that you end up in a nut house though) lol.

It's a special friendship that we have,

The way I make you smile and the way I make

you laugh,

You say that I crack you up,

Yup,

That, I love.

Than me, you've probably never met anyone

dafter,

Ours is a friendship full of fun and laughter,

Admit it though, it does make the day go faster,

Whether I'm telling a crap joke,

Or a funny story told when we've spoke,

Yup,

I love it that I can crack you up.

I hope we get to write many more fun chapters

filled with laughs and fun together,

I hope I continue "cracking you up" forever,

Yup.

Oh, how I love cracking you up.

I just love seeing you laugh,

I'm not good at much, but maybe that, I'm a little

bit good at,

And I love seeing you smile,

Making you smile, always makes me feel

worthwhile,

Yup,

I love it that I can crack you up.

Yep, buddy,

So I promise thee,

To never stop trying,

Keeping you laughing and smiling,

And yup,

To keep cracking you up.

So promise me,

To never lose your laugh and beautiful smile,

matey,

Because yup,

I love cracking you up.

Little Games

No. 26

Khadijah, just a quick poem which will hopefully make you smile as you trawl the memory bank. Remember when we go out dinner time and we sit on our bench by the clock with a sandwich or something, we have a chat about anything and everything, we've put the world to rights sat on there ain't we buddy a couple of times and we watch the world go by, wondering what people are doing and why aren't they working like us. (They can't all be on annual leave!) I still remember when I said to you shall we play a game? It was that one where we see people walking past and guess their names as we'd take it in turns and say she looks like a Karen (Because there is always one) lol, he looks like a Steve etc etc and we briefly tried lookalikies too where we have to try and spot celebrity lookalikes. We definitely had a good laugh. Will have to do it again soon matey but perhaps somewhere like a coffee shop or wine bar for the professional/posh type lookalike and the name guessing game too see if we get any Percivals or Tarquin's or any other posh names we can think of. But yeah, it was great spending time with you outside of the office, I enjoyed it and it was fun and a laugh and I hope you enjoyed it too and made you smile.

Walking into Town,

We find our little bench by the clock and we sit
down,
Seeing what Willenhall has to offer … We're
disappointed, it's not a lot,
Paris, Milan, L.A, Monaco, St Tropez it is not,
We have a chat,
About this and that,
Anything,
And Everything,
Topics, serious and not so,
Oh how I wish time didn't go so fast and went a
little more slow,
I could talk to you for hours, I just feel so
comfortable with you,
I'm just like an open book, It's like for forever
you, I have knew,
For me to be able to talk personal stuff, feelings,
emotions stuff with you, is testament to you,
I struggle to talk about that stuff,
But with you I never shut up!
I just feel so at ease and comfortable with ya,

You're a one in a billion special kinda person

Khadijah,

It's funny,

You and me,

Sitting there on the bench probably looking like

Forrest Gump and Jenny,

Chatting just like in the movie,

Minus the box of choccies,

I'll remember for next time, you just name the

brand, Milk Tray? Cadburys?

We sit and watch the world go by,

We see people walking about not at work and we

wonder why?

Then we remember and say oh, we're in

Willenhall,

It's like a moment of clarity as we say look

around, there is sod all,

We wonder what are they doing?

And where are they going?

But definitely our most favourite of games,

Is guess the names,

Always a laugh,

As we say she looks like she'd be called a Kath,

Ooh look over there, definitely a Pete,

Drinking a bottle of Whiskey neat,

And Karen, there is always a Karen,

And a chavvy kid, he's gotta be a Darren,

Of silly fun games we have quite the selection,

Guess the names, guess the job, they're in the

collection,

Oh and lookalikies

Where we try and spot people who look like

celebrities,

Didn't we once say good grief,

It's Kim Kardashian without teeth!

It's a great one hour of the afternoon,

Sadly it goes all to soon,

But for me, with you, that time spent,

Is truly a magic moment,

So Khadijah, this lovely friend of mine,

I look forward to playing again soon some time.

Winner, Winner, Khadijah

No. 27

Khadijah, just a quick poem to toast your two victories at the Gym Class you told me about (should have been a clean sweep of three if not for crooked refereeing in the last event) lol. Bless you being modest playing down your success saying it was not that impressive if I'd seen the others in the class. No, no, ruthless like I said, remember you said I cracked you up when I said remember our conversation about here teaching kids it's the taking part that counts and the kids getting a prize for 10th place when other countries in sport obviously don't accept anything less than first place, they teach the kids that only winning counts, we teach them its ok to fail and finish in the quarter finals or something. You laughed when I said at school sports day I deliberately waited to race the fat kids knowing I would win to get maximum points for my house team and also used the analogy of like a lion in the wild hunting will target the weak buffalo or whatever it fancies for dinner to maximize the chance of success. Celebrate your win, big yourself up, you could only beat what was in front of you matey, a win is a win.

You did make me laugh and smile with your tales

of the gym,

When you told me of your impressive win,

Two out of three ain't bad, (there's a song lyric
there)

In the other event you were robbed and I'm
raging mad,

Crooked refereeing,

To stop you winning,

That's what I'm surmising,

Bloody jealousy,

If you ask me,

Is it your fault you're too damn good, man!

I know I'm bias, being your biggest fan,

Me,

I demand a stewards enquiry,

You said I made you smile when I sent you that
gif of Jack saying run Rose,

You know I would've been cheering you on,

bragging as you left them for dust, saying there
she goes,

My friend Rose,

I would have cheered you on so loud,

Of you, I'm very proud,

But you being you, so down to earth and modest,

Said "It's not that big an achievement if you saw

who I was up against if I'm honest"

But Khadijah,

Remember one of our many conversations? No,

then here's a reminder,

We were putting the world to rights when we said

here they say its not about winning but taking

part as we said nonsense second is just first loser,

We commented its like teaching kids to accept

failure,

I crack you up, I remember you say,

As I told you about me picking the opportune

moment to race the fat kids at school sports day,

I said I did it deliberately,

To give my house team maximum points for

victory,

I also used the lion hunting the weak for prey

analogy,

Moments like this for me will be a precious

memory,

Of this interaction between you and me,

So for winning matey don't feel guilty,

So I say in your winners glory, bask,

You kicked ass,

Celebrate it, after all you can only beat what's in

front of ya,

Khadijah,

Look at me playing role of your own personal

cheerleader,

At poms-poms and wearing a skirt though I draw

the line,

A skirt? Not with these legs of mine,

Hope that brought a smile to your face,

Or are laughing to yourself as you read this mate,

So on your victories I say well done,

But wherever you would have come,

In my eyes you would always be number one!

ME CHEERING YOU ON WHATEVER
YOU DO!

Fish & Chips

No. 28

Khadijah, you'll probably remember me telling you about Winston meowing at me for a bit of fish and me calling him a little twat, I recall it made you laugh. Well thanks again from me and Winston for dinner and tea and the next one is on me matey. The service wasn't the best but the company was the best. It was funny spending the rest of the afternoon dodging interrogation by the office PC. Lol. Anyway, Thanks again.

At a loose end sitting at my desk one lunchtime,

When, came an invite out to dinner which one

cannot decline,

My lovely friend Khadijah,

Asking if I fancied grabbing some dinner,

Her treat,

I tried to say I'll get this,

But she did insist,

I said well it's my turn next time,

She said fine,

I knew it was futile to try and argue as her I

wouldn't beat,

Morrisons Café it was for Fish and Chips,

The service left a lot to be desired … not the

quickest,

But the company was the very best,

I was truly blessed,

Though time wasn't our friend,

So we took what we couldn't finish in boxes in

the end,

So that would later be my tea,

And that's where this gets funny,

As when at home I was serving,

I heard this purring,

Looking up at me was Winston, my cat,

The look on his face, you knew he was saying

what's that?

He was licking his lips,

As I said Fish and chips,

His meows got louder and louder,

I tried to ignore him save to say no, this is my

Tea, you've had yours, this is off my friend

Khadijah,

He meowed some more, louder each time,

The look on his face as if to say where's mine?

Meow, meow, the fish, I want some of that,

Tiresome of the meows I broke some off and said

here you little twat,

I gave him a warning, saying don't expect this

every week off Auntie Khadijah,

Will ya?

So to my lovely friend Khadijah, I once again

thank you for dinner and tea,

Until next time when the next lunch is on me.

P.S Thanks too from Winnie. (Winston)

Song Lyrics, Annotations and Movie Quotations

No. 29

Khadijah, I love our friendship, the quirkiness, uniqueness, the fun we have, some might even say crazy or daft but they don't get it, wouldn't get it, they're not us.

I love our little Jack and Rose thing we have, you know having each other's back and being there for each other, it's really special, I value it so much, I'll touch on this in more detail in another poem dedicated to us being like Jack and Rose so won't go into massive detail here and spoil that poem.

The quirkiness comes from our conversations we have and how we can always seem to relate a movie quote or song lyric to it or the situation, like remember when you were studying for your exam, and you were really worried, stressed about it even doubted that you'd be able to do it, and I told you how much I believed in you, how amazing, brilliant, clever you are and that you can do it, you will do it, you need to believe in yourself because I believe in you buddy, I remember saying to you, "In the words of George Michael, you gotta have faith", as I then went on to say you'll smash it mate. Then from there I think Jack and Rose followed around the same time possibly before, as I said remember just like Jack and Rose in Titanic, if there is anything I can do to help, or take some of the stress off you, just let me know, Jack has your back! Of course we have the you jump, I jump too as I've told you I'll always be here for you no matter what matey, like you've been there for me countless times, (bloody hell, I'm sounding like the friends theme tune now! Lol)

There is many, many more no doubt, but I wanted to cover the main two in the poem, our friend George Michael and Jack and Rose as they are the ones that really define our quirky friendship with their lyrics and quotes and play a massive part in our amazing, beautiful, wonderful friendship.

We have a friendship unique and quirky,

Don't we?,

Whatever our conversations,

We can always find a way to relate movie

quotations,

Whatever topic,

Yep, for that too, we have a song lyric,

Song lyrics or movie quotations,

For all manner of discussions,

And all manner of situations,

One of our most used song lyrics was from our

friend George Michael of Wham,

Brought out when you was studying for your

exam,

To help remind you how amazing and great you

am,

How the exam you will breeze,

You're brilliant, you'll pass with ease,

If, in yourself, you just believe,

I remember I told you I believed in you,

But you knew,

That line we did used to say, - "You Gotta have

faith", mate,

As I tried to encourage you and tell you that you

were great,

As I tried to support you when you were in a "I

can't do this", stressed state,

As I Would say "Yes you can",

Am I really going to go there with a Bob the

Builder quote, man?

Listen to George Michael, I would joke,

A truer word he's never spoke,

As I would say, remember like George's other song,

He's not wrong,

Remember if you need anything, "Mark's your man!"

You'd smile and say thank you,

As I'd say anything, you know that, if there is anything I can do,

Like the Bryan Adams song, "I'll do it for you",

But moving on from a song lyric,

To quotes from the movie Titanic,

A film everyone knows,

Me and you, have our own little friendship thing,

Jack and Rose,

As whenever I can do something for you to help,

I say Rose, just like Jack,

Remember, I have your back,

Jack and Rose, remember, you jump, I jump,

You smile as I then remind you how when we go

into town and sit on our bench, we must look like

Jenny and Forrest Gump,

There are obviously countless other examples that

I've missed,

But there's probably too many to list,

It always makes me smile does our unique, quirky,

friendship,

Our sense of humour, that others probably

wouldn't get it,

Probably wouldn't get our use of movie

quotations or a song lyric,

But that's a good thing, It's just our special thing,

the Jack and Rose dynamic,

I love our friendship,

I love our conversations,

How we always find a way to relate movie

quotations,

Or a music lyric.

Tea

No. 30

Khadijah, this poem was inspired by Tea. I guess what started it was when it came to mind when I remembered about you preparing for your exam and I know you were stressed and nervous etc. etc. about the exam and understandably so and you might recall me trying to encourage you and tell you you'll be great, you're do great and all the gotta have faith a 'la George Michael's song etc. etc. Also you'd just had that racing heart episode and so that dinnertime I went out and come back armed with a selection of teas and my little post-it notes made you smile and hopefully brightened up your day too. The one tea the heart tea, I wrote on the post-it especially for that big heart of yours, the tea is supposed to be good for the heart and after yours was racing I thought it might help plus I've told you before how big your heart is, how you are the most sweetest, most loveliest human I've ever, ever met how you always put others first above yourself, you're so selfless and God, how I wish the world was full of you's, what a special wonderful world it would be, but, I guess if the world had more you's then there would be no need for heaven because we'd already be there with such an amazing, lovely, sweet, selfless, kind human being as you around. I recall you smiled as I told you we had to look after that big

146

heart of yours.

There was that tea for the tummy, it looked like a urine sample, didn't taste much better than it looked either did it! I brought it and put a post it on it saying for the tummy to settle any nerves ahead of the exam.

There was a tea for brain power not that you needed much of a boost in that department, you're so smart and clever Khadijah.

Tiredness and Fatigue, there was a tea for that too if I recall correctly I guess just to try and help get you through your revision and study with an energy boost and lastly there was one called calm tea and again I think I wrote on the post-it note, to help you de-stress and calm any nerves etc. as I told you, you would be fine and would do great. I told you that unfortunately a dummy like me couldn't help you with your studies or with any answers but if I can encourage you and help you prepare by helping you de-stress or get you a boost in energy be it tea or biscuits etc. then I would.

Anyway enough rambling I guess and I'll just let you get on and read the poem. Lol. You could read this as you wait for the kettle to boil how long this intro is. Lol.

Khadijah,

What flavour?

147

What takes your fancy today?

Eh?

In your drawer,

You've got them all,

There's a tea for all occasions,

For all situations,

I would bring you various teas during your exam

preparations,

I'm picturing it now in my mind,

You saying in Mr T's voice as I bring you another

kind,

I picture you saying in his voice, "What tea is this

sucka?"

As I laugh and say "Such and such tea for when

you have your next cuppa".

A selection of teas I would go and get you,

All different and all different kinds of jobs they

do.

A previous favourite was the "Hearty" heart tea,

Number one choice until you made a recent new

discovery,

Recommended by your friend,

A delicious tasting green tea, pineapple blend,

The heart tea I brought to make you smile with

my little post-it note,

As I wrote,

Heart tea for and to look after that big, sweet,

heart of yours,

Different teas, you had quite a selection in your

drawers,

You know I'm like an elephant, I don't forget

anything you tell me,

See, I care about you, see,

Like the time you told me you felt queasy and

dodgy,

An upset tummy,

So out I went and got a suitable tea,

Said on the box especially for the tummy,

Of the other teas, this wasn't the most yummy,

Drinkable,

Looked a bit like a urine sample,

Mint and fennel,

To help your tummy settle,

"Something to help settle nerves and your

tummy", I wrote,

On another little post-it note,

Then there was a tea called "Brainy"

Brought to help boost you with your study,

Not that you needed a boost in brain power,

You're so smart and clever,

Then there was the tea for tiredness and fatigue

to give you a boost in energy,

To help get you through your hours upon hours

of study,

The teas were just my daft way of trying to help,

feel useful I guess,

Try and help you feel better and de-stress,

With your drawers full of teas, several varieties of

teas, you're the tea girl of the office,

With a selection of teas of all flavours and for all

purposes,

Fruity and healthy,

In your drawer you've got the tea,

Miss Twinnings or Miss Tetley is what we'll have

to start calling you,

Having as many varieties of teas as you do,

Oh our Khadijah,

Oh how she does love a good cuppa.

Vitamins

No. 31

Khadijah, lets talk vitamins!

Well, we talk about anything and everything in our chats don't we, from putting the world to rights, to health, anything really and this poem was inspired by how you know how I constantly tell you how you brighten my day etc. I thought about the conversation we had some months back, outside it was pissing with rain, we were in your office and talking about how expensive it is to be healthy, dentist prices, optician prices, waiting lists unless you go private etc., etc. and the lack of vitamin D in the country because we don't get enough sun here, I can still see your beautiful smile now when I said I don't have that problem, the sun shines everyday in my world, you make the sun shine everyday, you always brighten my day. You said aww, bless ya, but it's true I always just feel so happy whenever I'm around you or in your company. Anyway you'll see in this book there is a whole poem dedicated to you making the sun shine everyday in my world which goes into more detail. I hope you like it.

And this will probably sound corny but I'll say it anyway buddy, you have a gift of knowing when I'm not myself but you always know how to make me smile and feel better and it's called vitamin U (you).

You and me,

Have had many a chat about being healthy,

The importance of healthy food and eating your

greens,

Getting enough of your vital vitamins,

You know the sort of things we say,

But I get my main two vitamins everyday,

We all know vitamin D from sunshine,

You'll recall our chat when you said in this

Country we don't see enough sun to get adequate

Vitamin D,

I made you smile when I said everyday, the sun, I

see,

As I told you that with you around I'm basking in

permanent sunshine in this world of mine,

With you about, the day,

It's never ever grey,

As bright as the sun was your beautiful, sweet

smile,

And meanwhile,

Whenever I'm feeling blue,

To cheer me up you just know what to do,

You know what I need, what vitamin will make

me feel better,

And Khadijah,

Like a miracle cure,

For sure,

It's vitamin U,

Nothing or no-one can make me feel better, feel

happy, like you do!

When Your Heart Races, My Heart Races

No. 32

Khadijah, I remember in the run up to your exam and you had a lot going on as well as your revision and you'd been up A&E with a racing heart, I of course asked how you were and are you sure you're ok that sort of thing, because I care etc. You said you were at home and your heart was pounding so you went to A&E to get checked out. I asked if your parents went with you, you said no, you didn't want them to know because they would worry and you didn't want them worrying. Bless you huh, see always, always putting others first before you and thinking of others, you and that big beautiful sweet heart of yours, what am I going to do with you huh? We can't change you and you'll never change you're just that kind of caring kind person and I wouldn't want to change you anyway, it's one of the qualities I love about you, what am I talking about, I love everything about you, you're you, the kindest most sweetest person I've ever met. I do wish though sometimes you'd put yourself first matey.

Anyway let's get back on track with the story, you said you went alone to A&E and waited hours to be seen, I said mate, you should have

called, I would have come up and sat with you save you being on your own, I know how boring those places can be when you're waiting for hours, I would have kept you company, someone to talk to or just to sit with, share the boredom. You smiled and said no don't be silly, I couldn't do that, I said you can, I don't mind, I would have come, I'm always awake anyway as I don't sleep so might as well do something lol. We laughed. I said seriously, I'm only down the road, I would have gotten a taxi up to sit with you.
You said thanks that's really sweet bless you.

We discussed what could have caused it, the stress of the impending exam, revision, other stuff going on, I said be careful, it's your bodies warning to try and relax and take it easy stop being at everyone's beck and call and take time for yourself because if you don't you'll burn out and these things can lead to heart attacks. I told you about what my Doctor said to me when I went with chest pain. I said look, I know it's hard for you, because it's not who you are, it's not the person you are, you are the most selfless person I have ever met, how you put everyone first before you, how you do things for everyone else and have no time for yourself, how you're there for everyone else but when you need people to be there for you no-one is there. I told you for what its worth, if you ever need someone to be there for you, to talk to, just listen to you, cry on, whatever, then I'm always here, I may not be your first choice, probably not even in your first million choices but if you get desperate, I'm here, I'll always be here, if I'm your last choice, well I'd rather be your last choice than no choice.

You also mentioned the Red Bull you had been drinking the previous day and said you were going to lay off it for a bit, we agreed it was probably wise. That was probably this idiot's fault as I brought them large cans and there was too much in them they were the only ones they had left and you had been in need of an energy boost.

Dinnertime I went out and come back with a selection of teas as I brought you some Heart Tea, De-Stress, tummy and brain tea (brain tea sounds disgusting brain power boosting tea I should say) lol. I showed you the heart tea and put a little post it note on saying to help look after the big thing of yours, your heart which made you smile. I of course kept checking you were okay whenever I'd go past your office it probably must have gotten annoying for you but just wanted to make sure my buddy was okay.

I remember you saying sorry,

When you didn't text our goodnight text that we

do nightly,

You'd been up A&E,

An issue to do with cardiology,

I told you about the missed text, not to worry,

For anything, you don't need to be sorry,

I said as long as you're feeling better is the main
thing,

You said you'd been up A&E hours waiting,

I said who went with you? Did your parents go?

You said no,

You went alone,

I said oh mate, you should have rang me on the
phone,

I would have came up and sat with you save you
being on your own,

I said I've been in enough Hospitals recently,

To know how boring they can be,

Waiting around for hours and hours for someone
to see,

I would have come and kept you company,

You said oh no, don't be silly,

I said matey,

I'm only down the road, It's no inconvenience for

me,

You said why your parents didn't go with you,

You didn't want to worry them so they never

knew,

You said your heart had been racing,

I said it's probably all the s$%t and stress you'd

been facing,

When your heart races, mine races too,

As I worry about you,

I said take it easy,

You know where I am matey,

If you need me,

You said it could have been the large Red Bull

Energy Drink,

You said, you were going to lay off it you think,

You said it could have been the Red Bull that

made your heartbeat enhance,

We both said it's best not take the risk, not worth

the chance,

Dinnertime, I went into the town,

I came back and said look what I found,

Heart Tea,

A safer alternative to Red Bull Energy,

You looked and smiled and I said, we have to

look after that massive heart of yours don't we!

It was delicious and fruity,

I said we have to keep that big heart of yours

healthy,

I joked because of how big your heart is it must

be heavy,

How you're so selfless and put others first,

As I told you its one of your best qualities but

also your worst,

As you are bloody important too,

I for one think the world of you!

But me telling you that is nothing new,

We said it was probably caused by worry,

And exam anxiety,

I said for you I know it's hard, but put yourself

first and take it easy,

I said if there is anything I can do,

Let me know, I'll help you,

Thinking about it this might have been the time I

brought the Calm and De-Stress teas too,

A various selection to try and help you,

You said thanks for this,

I said no problem Miss,

Remember Rose and Jack,

I've got your back!

I said take it easy again, listen to your body, it's

saying relax,

Or next time it could be a heart attack,

You will no doubt recall,

That every time I walked past your office, I'd

stick my head through the door,

"Are you ok?" Yes, I'd then say, "are you sure?"

It'd must have annoyed you after a while as I'd

keep asking if you were okay,

Yes, thanks for checking on me you'd say,

But you know I care deeply about you as I said no

problem, if you need anything let me know,

As back downstairs to work I'd go,

I was just relieved you were fine and hoped you

knew,

That it's because I care so much about you that I

kept checking on you.

You Almost Gave Me A Heart Attack

No. 33

Khadijah, just a poem about that time you tried to kill me off! Lol (just joking) but you did give me a scare, making my heart thump, pound and race for a different reason other than being in your company. Yep when you text me saying "Mark, help" I tell you I felt ill, I felt the colour drain from my face, I probably went white as a ghost, I thought something bad had happened or you'd had an accident, you did text again immediately after to say all it was, was that you had arrived on the car park early but because I was still typing a response to the S.O.S this idiot didn't see that did he, lol, I was texting to say what's happened, are you ok? I'm on my way, that sort of thing, this was the times where every morning we were meeting about 8.30ish on the car park as you had forgotten your keys and we'd meet so I could let you in.

As is typical it would have to be the morning that the bus was late and seemingly every stop an idiot would get on not having their fare ready or know where they wanted to go and added to the delays as I was shaking my head and muttering to myself for fuck sake, come on, just get on the bus. Why don't you have your money ready.

We laughed as I told you because of the above, at one point I contemplated getting off the bus and running to you as I thought it'd be quicker.

You apologised for scaring me and called yourself an idiot, I said no need to apologise I'm just glad you're ok, and I told you you're not an idiot, you're anything but, you're amazing, the most amazing person I've ever met. I'm sorry for overthinking and thinking the worst, it's just I care so much about you buddy. I told you if you were in trouble or ever needed me for anything, I'd be there, anytime, anywhere, I'd always somehow find a way of getting there you know that. We laughed again about our Jack and Rose connection, you jump, I jump, Jack has your back thingy majig because I know it makes you laugh when I say thingy majig.

It was 11th July 2023,

When you text me,

It was a little early,

Not the time you'd text normally,

And when I read it,

Well, I panicked,

Colour drained from my face,

My heart began to race,

164

Beating at such a frantic pace,

For you it usually does when I see you, this heart

of mine,

But the reason was different this time,

I thought you were in danger,

And my mind was saying God, don't let anything

bad have happened to Khadijah,

More than anything or anyone, I bloody care

about her,

The message read, "Mark, help", it gave me a

heart scare,

Thought I was in some sort of nightmare,

Some sort of hell,

When I thought with you all was not well,

My heart began to pound,

Worried you were not safe and sound,

Scared something had happened to you,

All kinds of thoughts my mind went through,

Thank fully what you sent next,

The next text,

Which at first I didn't see,

As me replying to your S.O.S, kept my fingers
busy,
Something along the lines on his way is Jack,
Jack has your back,
Our private little thing between us is likening us
to Jack and Rose,
For those who don't knows,
Thankfully after reading your second text after I
sent my reply, my worry eased,
As in that second text, you confirmed all it was,
was that you had arrived too early, I was pleased,
It was the time you had just forgot your keys,
So every morning, on the car park we had been
meeting,
And we'd enter the office together after a chat
and our morning greeting,
I was just relieved there was no cause for alarm,
I was just relieved that you hadn't come to any
harm,
For scaring me, you said sorry,
I told you not to worry,

I said you gave my heart palpitations and a scare,

I said it's because about you I deeply care,

You said you were such an idiot,

I said don't be silly, you're not,

I made you smile though,

As I said I contemplated getting off the bus and

running to your rescue like Jack,

As the morning traffic was so bad,

And mate,

It would just happen to be the day the bus was

late!

I told you if something had happened I would

have got there,

By hook or by crook, by any means possible, I

don't care,

Anyplace, anytime, anywhere,

For you,

There is nothing I would not do,

We smiled as I said Rose, you gave Jack a heart

attack,

But Jack would have come, Jack has your back,

And I do too,

I'll always be here for you,

Past, present, future,

Then, now, forever,

For you, beautiful, amazing, special Khadijah.

I'll Meet You On The Car Park

No. 34

Khadijah, take no notice of the title, I'm not challenging you to a fight lol. You'd knock me out! No this is about our morning ritual when I'll meet you on the car park usually a little after half past eight and we'll walk the few yards from your car to the front door but in that time we have a pre-work chat usually about whether we had good evenings, did your revision go ok or did we sleep well. It's always my favourite way to start the day and you know how much I kick myself for letting you down if because of the buses I'm late and miss our chat, of course you always say don't worry, it's ok but you should see me seething on the bus if I see the time is ticking on and I'm miles away and some idiot gets on the bus without having their fare ready or know where they are going so delays the bus for a few minutes, I'm shaking my head and thinking I'm gonna miss my chat with my mate now you prick.

The title doesn't necessarily sound right,

If you didn't read on you could be forgiven for

thinking it was about two blokes arranging to

fight,

But no,

That's not how this poem does go,

Every morning a little after half past eight,

On the car park, I meet my mate,

I greet her as she gets out the car,

To go to the office front door, we haven't got far,

But in just those few yards we have our pre-work

chat,

You know, how was our evenings and did we

sleep well and that,

We haven't got far to go to the front door,

But this morning ritual for me means it's a great

start to the day for sure,

But should I be late,

Because of the buses I kick myself and hate to let

down my mate,

She always says not to worry, it's okay,

But on my mind it does play,

As I miss my favourite way to start the day.

I'll Meet You At The Bottom Of The Staircase

No. 35

Khadijah, always one of the most heartwarming moments of the day for me is this, home time, I like to think we care about each other and I love our friendship how we look out for each other and clearly care about each other as every night when we leave, we always tell each other to get home safely, I just think its so lovely how we text to say yep, home safe and sound and hope you are too. Stupid me getting emotional writing this, silly fool ain't I? Yeah, and waiting for you at the bottom of the stairs I do feel like Jack and then you come down the stairs smiling, I don't know why but it makes me smile too, it's just a lovely memory I'll forever treasure. This little home time ritual we have always warms my heart and guarantees I go home smiling so thank you again matey.

Like Jack and Rose,

Another Scene everyone knows,

You know which one I mean,

The grand staircase scene,

It's just gone five o'clock and in a scene

reminiscent,

Like Jack I'm stood at the bottom of the stairs

waiting, being patient,

The smile on my face,

As you come down the staircase,

You remind me of Rose, always dressed elegantly,

A beautiful young lady,

At the bottom of the stairs I'm there to greet you,

As the working day is through,

We leave together and have a little chat,

Wishing each other a lovely evening and to get

home safely and that,

As I make the promise to send our nightly text

good night,

And wish each other sweet dreams and to sleep

tight,

For tomorrow soon comes around and come the

end of the day where again we'll meet at the same

place,

At the bottom of the staircase.

KHADIJAH, THIS SCENE REMINDS ME
OF
WHEN WE WOULD MEET AT THE END
OF
THE DAY. ME AT THE BOTTOM OF
THE
STAIRCASE – OUR JACK & ROSE THING
– I'VE

SAID BEFORE HOW YOU REMIND ME

OF ROSE

COMING DOWN THE STAIRS –

ELEGANCE & CLASS.

Get Home Safely

No. 36

Khadijah, I spoke to you the other day about this, this memory, the time I was about to go to the Post Office and as usual it was raining. You told me to be careful and watch I don't slip, it was very wet, it's funny, I smiled all the way to the post office, I was just so touched by your concern and care and then as we left at home time and we was having our usual chat on the car park, you know the usual have a good evening etc. when you told me to get home safely and to text you when I did just to let you know I was ok, I was really moved and touched, I know I've said it before and get so emotional when I think about it, but you really are the most sweetest, most loveliest human I have ever, ever met. I told you recently, you're like a guardian angel the way you look out for me, what to you may seem like a throw away comment "Get home safe" to me, it touched my heart, It reminded me of something Mum would say to me, or Dad when I was out on the weekend, he'd always say stay safe and get home safe and always wanted me to text him to let him know I was ok. So, Khadijah, thank you, thank you for everything, thank you for being you, the sweetest, the loveliest person I know, I just really hope you get your happy ever after in life because you deserve it matey, I hope life starts being good to you and you get all the nice lovely things you deserve and all the happiness in the world because you are one of life's diamonds and you deserve to shine. You have such a big heart, I wish there were more you's in this world, this world would be such a better place if there was matey, I guess I'm lucky, my world is beautiful because you are in it so I'm blessed.

You're the sweetest most caring person I know,

It's raining outside as I'm about to go to the Post

Office as you say "mind how you go",

"Watch you don't slip, it's very wet and slippery",

I will, thanks for worrying about me,

That's what I say,

As I then head on my way,

Shortly after, home time comes and as we say our

goodbyes on the car park,

You say, Mark,

Get home safe,

It warms my heart and soul and brings a smile to

my face,

As you say text me,

Let me know you got home safely,

I say I will do,

I get home and I text you, I promised and I'd

never break a promise to you,

The text goes something like home safe and

sound, hope you did too,

Matey,

I'm so lucky,

Lucky to have someone like you look out for and

care about me,

Wanting to make sure I get home safely,

Never in my life have I met someone as

incredible as you, someone so lovely,

I'm truly blessed to have a friend like you, you're

such a sweetie,

Clearly,

We care about each other deeply,

But buddy,

I guess that's just what friends do,

You look out for me and I look out for you.

Night, Night, Sleep Tight, Sweet Dreams

No. 37

Khadijah, a short poem about our nightly ritual, where we will text each other night, night around the usual time ish of 10p.m. You hopefully know I care very deeply for you mate, what I probably never told you is that as I say my prayers at night, I pray that God watches over you and looks after you, I ask him to send a Guardian Angel to look out for you, not just any Guardian Angel though, I ask him to send my Mum and Dad as I know that they are watching over me and would know how important I value you so not just any Guardian Angels would do for this assignment mate.

Every night around 10ish, we text,

Wishing each other good rest,

As we say night, night,

Sleep tight,

I wish her sweet dreams,

As I then pray to God to watch over her and send

a Guardian Angel to keep her safe please.

I Pray, Lord Look After Her

No. 38

Khadijah, this is something I do every day and every night … pray. Yes, every morning, every night and sometimes in between I pray to the Lord, pray to him to look after you, to keep you safe and to send a Guardian Angel to look after you. I do have a prayer I say to him every night that I made up, I know it off by heart, it's sort of become a ritual, maybe one day I'll share it with you.

I know, I know, you'll probably telling me don't worry about you, I can hear your voice in my head as I write this telling me that, but I do worry, I guess because I truly do care about you buddy. I guess it's why I ask the good Lord to watch over you and send you a Guardian Angel to watch over you. I think I've told you before, maybe or maybe not, but I do ask him to send my Mum and Dad to watch over you to keep you safe, I guess because I trust them, I know if somehow they were listening they would, they would do it for me, they'd know how special I think you are and therefore would make sure you're ok for me, I know they'd like you, and this I know that I have told you before, but when I do speak to Mum and Dad, be it at the cemetery or elsewhere, I do tell them about you, how amazing I think you are and always ask them make sure you're ok for me and to keep you safe.

I told you in one of our conversations before about that YouTube video I had watched before about signs that those who have passed on are communicating to say they are ok/made it to the other side and that they are watching over you and one of those was when they send someone into your life but we'll touch on that a lot more in one of the other poems in this book but you probably know what I'm on about if you remember our conversation about it. If not the other poem will jog your memory.

He's only a prayer away,

Every night and day,

Mine I do say,

As to him I pray,

I ask the good Lord to do me a favour,

And to look after her,

Her being Khadijah,

And Khadijah, to watch over,

To keep Khadijah safe and well,

To send her a guardian Angel,

And to Khadijah, please bless her,

With nothing but happiness now and forever.

Dream Man, Say Hello To Your Biggest Fan …

No. 39

Khadijah, you'll remember this, I remember it well.

I remember when I told you I did something daft, you looked at me and said what have you done? I told you that I know Jason Statham is your dream man (lucky him) lol and I wanted to try and do something memorable, something special for you, and as usual with me, unique and different, as I told you, I messaged him on Instagram asking him for an autograph for you or even just a reply to my message saying hello Khadijah, love Jason or something like that, something that would have made you smile and probably have been treasured forever by you etc.

You called me mad for attempting this as you smiled.

I said I would let you know if I hear anything. I remember updating you daily saying sorry, still nothing from Jason. I said he was probably filming or the time difference between here and the U.S might be why he hadn't responded but a few more days passed without reply. I remember you saying it's okay, he's probably

181

busy with his stunning supermodel girlfriend Rosie. I remember making you smile as I said yeah, but if he saw you, he'd soon drop her for you, you said no, it's okay as I said anyone would be lucky to have you, they'd be the luckiest person in the world, as I told you, you could have anyone you wanted as you said aww you're sweet, bless ya.

A few more days passed as I then told you I'd made another attempt with a follow up message as I said I'll probably end up blocked or have my account suspended but if I did, Winston would start from his account which made you laugh. I told you this second message would probably be a last attempt at pulling this off for risk of being banned or blocked as you said don't worry about it.

Well here we are at the book now and sadly he still hasn't responded and I'm gutted matey as I know how much it would have meant to you and how much it would have made you smile. I do feel like I let you down not being able to pull this off for you even though I knew it was a very long, long shot of being successful.

Anyway sorry again buddy I failed.

.

Snubbed,

By Mr Hollywood,

Not one but two,

Two messages ignored by you,

How could ya?,

How dare ya, ignore my mate Khadijah,

Jason Statham, have you gone crackers lad?

Are you mad?

What's wrong with you man?

She's your biggest fan!

You're her dream man!

I sent you two messages on Instagram,

Asking for an autograph or even just a reply

saying hello,

That would have done, so Khadijah, I could

show,

It would have put a big smile on her face,

She would've been jumping for joy all over the

place,

It would have probably taken pride of place on

the wall of her office,

To have been able to have done something

special like this for her was my wish,

But over my plan, my hopes you had to s###t,

As you ignored my messages,

Messing up this,

She would have been smiling from ear to ear,

It's something she would have treasured and held

so very dear,

It would have meant the world to her,

My beautiful friend Khadijah,

If only I could have pulled this off for her,

It would have made her day,

But you had to go and let her down Eh!

To try and make her happy and smile I'll try

anything,

An autograph or an hello would to her, of meant

everything,

For attempting this, she called me mad,

As I said Khadijah, I just wanted to make you

glad,

If I could've pulled it off,

But I did tell her it was a long shot,

I knew what it would have meant to her,

My beautiful, amazing friend, Khadijah,

It would have really made her smile,

All the effort would have been so worthwhile,

And I also told her, that I would let her know if

by some miracle I heard back,

After a few days of nothing, I joked as I told her,

don't worry, you've always got Jack!

Jason doesn't know what he's missing buddy,

She said to me, it's okay,

As defending you, she did say,

She did say you were probably too busy,

With supermodel girlfriend Rosie,

Or shooting a movie,

And no disrespect mate,

I'm sure Rosie's great,

But I'm telling ya,

She don't compare to my beautiful, amazing

friend Khadijah,

If you saw her, if you ever met her,

It'd be, Rosie, see ya!

I'm off with someone much, much better,

The best ever, the most beautiful girl ever,

Khadijah!

To Khadijah, Rosie, don't compare to her!

As I type this poem, I contemplate whether to go

for third time lucky,

I can hear Khadijah in my head in her voice, now,

saying you're crazy,

Yep, that's me!

Yep, persevere like the character from that movie,

Shawshank Redemptions, Andy,

You know the scene, where he keeps writing

asking for books for the library,

Until they get fed up and cave into pressure,

Maybe if I persist I may get an autograph or an

hello for her,

Or most likely a block on Instagram and Twitter,

But that's ok, Winston the Cat will take my place

for Auntie Khadijah!

It'd be his way of thanking Auntie Khadijah for

his fish supper,

Khadijah, matey,

I've said this before, but I'm sorry,

I wasn't able to pull this off for ya,

Though I may reset,

And have another attempt yet!

I know it would have been special and meant a lot

to ya, Khadijah,

But Mr Big Time Hollywood Actor,

Ignored me on Instagram,

But I know despite it all, you're still his biggest

fan,

He's still your dream man,

If only he realised what he was missing and how

lucky he is eh,

Buddy!

To be adored by you,

If only he knew!

Hollywood Dream... You Look Just Like Marilyn Monroe

No. 40

Khadijah, it was a Friday evening and I was sleeping but recall a dream I had, you were in it, I guess that was obvious or else there wouldn't be a poem out of it would there!

I don't remember much of it as I woke up before finding out what happens in the end. You were clearly on my mind I suppose.

Now, I don't know if we were going to some sort of party or whatever but you were walking just in front, you looked just like Marilyn Monroe (we all know how she was regarded as one of the most beautiful women to have ever lived), (I know you don't think you are, or that you're nothing special, but you are, you are beautiful too, if only I could give you the power to see yourself through my eyes and I've got four of them lol, then you'd know what I mean matey. I know when we've had conversations and you've said such and such is beautiful, and I've told you that you are too and any guy would be the luckiest guy on God's green earth to have you, you put yourself down matey and you shouldn't because you're amazing, you're beautiful, you're funny, you're sweet, you're lovely, you're selfless, you put others first, you're so caring, I could go on and on but then this book would be never ending) Anyway, back to the dream, in the dream, you had your beautiful blonde hair styled like hers and was wearing that iconic white dress and I remember in the dream telling you three times that you looked absolutely gorgeous, you looked just like Marilyn Monroe, then sadly I must have woken up because that's all I remember of it.

I can't pretend to know why this dream came to me. I don't know, maybe I must have spent a lot of time with you that day so you were on my mind and maybe I must have been writing on my Marilyn calendar and that must have been in my mind somewhere and the stupid brain combined the two for a dream, who knows how the mind works. It was a nice dream though and obviously shows I do think of you matey. I must have been missing you being a Friday evening knowing I wouldn't see you again until the Monday so the mind must have compensated or something lol.

It was really weird was that night, because when I must have gotten back off to sleep you appeared in my dream again but it was different to this Marilyn one – I've done a short poem about that too which explains that one.

The mind is a funny thing and how it works I guess.

It was a Friday evening,

And I was sleeping,

I must have been dreaming,

Why, I do not know,

But I dreamt you were dressed like Marilyn

Monroe,

I don't remember much of it,

Just a little bit,

Unfortunately, I must have awoken,

Before the dreams conclusion,

I can remember from my mind,

That in the dream you were walking in front, and

I was a step behind,

Your blonde hair styled like Marilyn's

As ever looking the bees knees,

You was wearing that white iconic dress,

You looked like an absolute Goddess,

In the dream, I remember saying to you, you

know,

You look just like Marilyn Monroe,

Followed up by "you look absolutely gorgeous",

It suits you, does that white dress,

I don't know if I thought you were deaf as I said

it three times,

So clearly there was nothing wrong with my eyes,

And I certainly wasn't telling any lies,

Then, I must have woke from the dream,

Like I say, I don't know what it does mean,

I don't know if it was some sort of party,

That we were going to, you and me,

Who does know,

Why I dreamt you were dressed like Marilyn

Monroe,

I can't figure out why,

No matter how hard I try.

In The Field Of Dreams …

No. 41

Khadijah, this poem sort of follows on from the Marilyn one, where this was the second dream that night that you appeared in.

We were in some I think park at a street party (but on a field) type of thing or festival, I recall there being rows of tables, perhaps it was West Park or maybe and most likely Willenhall Park, you know that bit we walked past when we went one lunchtime with Lynsey, there.

In this dream I was some distance away and you were sitting down chatting to some young Irish guy or he was chatting to you, I glanced over and you saw me, I remember mouthing over, if, or shall, or can, I come over, and you smiling and beckoning me over saying please do, I guess I hesitated in just going straight over without asking as I wasn't sure if I was interrupting anything, thankfully I wasn't as you were relieved. I remember coming over and sitting in between you and he either turned to the next person and started talking to them or disappeared altogether, I don't recall. I just remember us sitting there and chatting, laughing, what we normally do buddy in each other's company. I remember you wore your hair down but again you was wearing a white dress just like you were in the Marilyn dream earlier that night, on reflection, I don't know if these two dreams were linked on that similar detail or indeed a continuation of the Marilyn dream, who knows. I do remember you sitting very prim and proper, like Royal and Regal or something, hands on your knees, back straight and we just chatted. I woke up then, not sure if I just woke or because the alarm went off for some reason.

Again, it was a lovely dream and again I can't pretend to know why you appeared in my dream I can only guess that because I cherish every moment spent with you during the day that the mind figured see her tonight too and knowing I wouldn't see you Saturday or Sunday and given that this was a Friday night thought spend some more time with her at some festival/street party (but in a field) but who knows, who am I to try and figure out or understand how minds work.

Not sure why I did poems about them actually, maybe to make you laugh I guess, but anyway.

It was still Friday evening,

And I was back sleeping,

About you, again I found myself dreaming,

Twice in one night, what's going on? First

Marilyn Monroe,

193

Now this, but again why? I do not know!

Again much of it I do not remember,

As I again must have awoken from my slumber,

Again I woke before it did conclude,

Who knows, maybe it's a dream in the future to

be continued?

The setting seemed to be in a park, maybe some

sort of street party (but in a field) or festival,

Perhaps West or Willenhall,

You had your golden blonde hair down, glowing

in the sun,

You were sitting next to someone,

I don't think by choice necessarily,

And me,

Was some distance away across this field,

I recall looking out, keeping my eyes peeled,

I did sigh,

When I saw you talking to this young Irish guy,

But on reflection, I think it was more him talking

to you,

And you being you, too polite to say go on, shoo,

I'd say he was probably only nineteen or twenty,

Chancing his arm with a girl so pretty,

As I looked over, I just happened to make eye

contact with ya,

I mouthed shall I come over?

You looked relieved as you beckoned with me

your hand,

Mouthing with your mouth, a command,

"Please do",

And so I made my way over and sat with you,

Sitting in between,

The Irish guy and thee,

He left our scene,

I guess thinking three's a crowd and two is

company,

So him being a spare part,

Did depart,

Or turned to the person next to us,

I don't really recall exactly, but I'm not fussed,

Us, it didn't bother,

We sat together,

Next to each other,

We just sat,

And was having a chat,

About what, I can't really recollect,

Maybe in the dream there was no clear dialect,

But replaying this dream in my mind, perhaps on
reflection,

With the Marilyn Monroe dream there is a
connection,

Perhaps this was some sort of continuation,

As again in this you were wearing a white dress,

Of course,

You looked gorgeous,

Like an absolute Goddess,

Your posture,

Prim and proper,

Hands on your knees and back straight,

As we just sat there and chatted mate,

And sadly this is the last I recall as then I must
have woke,

Or maybe, my sleep, the sound of the alarm

broke,

It was a lovely dream,

The sort of dream you never want to wake from

and dream forever, you know what I mean?

Perhaps it's my mind's way of telling me,

That when I'm all dreamy,

And in my dreams, you, I see,

That I really love and treasure your company,

And so subconsciously,

I'm thinking about thee.

Heart

No. 42

Khadijah, not so much a poem in the rhyming sense but wanted to get something like this in the book.

I couldn't write the book without mentioning your heart. I know we've discussed this, well, I've mentioned it to you, I've told you how you have the sweetest, most kindest heart, the warmest the biggest, the most selfless heart, how you always put others first before yourself, how you have always been there for me to talk to since day one of first meeting you. How you've helped me and got me through stuff I would never have gotten through if not for you buddy, how you've picked me up off the floor when I've been down. Well you know how you always make me smile and laugh everyday, how you make the sun shine everyday in my world. You're an amazing girl, do you know that? Have I told you before? Lol.

You're the most loveliest, most selfless human that I have ever, ever met. I know I'll never meet another you matey, you're a one off, you're the most special human I've ever been fortunate to meet.

Thank you for everything Khadijah.

Khadijah, you will always, always have a special place in my heart buddy. I promise I'll keep you safe in there forever.

Heart,

The biggest of hearts,

The kindest of hearts,

The warmest of hearts,

The sweetest of hearts,

The most selfless of hearts,

And you, - forever in my heart!

Her Smile

No. 43

Khadijah, a poem about your beautiful, bright smile.

I've told you countless times ain't I buddy about how you have such a beautiful smile.

Yep, just seeing you smile makes me smile, your smile has magical powers, I can't explain it but whenever I see you smile it makes me smile, it makes me feel happy, if ever I'm down just one of your beautiful bright smiles picks me up, it's funny, it's strange so thank you for always brightening my day and bless you, because you always have one for me.

You know I always try to return the favour and make you smile too, anyway I can, whether it's saying something funny, a note (well I say a note they end up as long as novels don't they!) lol, or doing something nice or out the ordinary (I'm never right am I? wired a bit different ain't I, unique, original, you could say as I try and do things a little more memorable than the norm so it means more). I hope this book makes you smile too buddy, though I did warn you it might, might if you're anything like this idiot writing it, cry, but hopefully good crying, if you know what I mean, ooh I'm an idiot I'm not explaining it very well am I? well, anyway, I hope you enjoy the book and it makes you smile at least once somewhere in here.

I know occasionally I've made you smile because you've told me I crack you up, it makes me laugh and smile when you say that, I'll keep trying to crack you up to keep that beautiful smile on your face matey. I love the fun and the laughs we have together and so dearly hope that we have many, many, many more chapters ahead of us yet buddy.

Anyway as this is a "Thank You, To Ya!", book, I'm going to thank you again here, thank you for always making me smile, being the reason I smile everyday and just being the most amazing, kind hearted, sweetest, most selfless, amazing (yes I know I've said that twice but you're so amazing I've said it twice lol) person that I have ever, ever met. So thank you buddy.

Please never ever lose your beautiful, bright smile matey, I hope you never ever lose that smile, I for one will always try to make you smile if I can, as often as I can, like you always make me smile.

Keep smiling and shining bright like the star that you are!

Her smile,

For one I'd walk a million mile,

Her smile as bright as the sun,

Her smile, I'll do anything to see one,

Her smile beautiful and bright,

Her smile, my day's highlight,

Her smile, if only she knew,

Her smile, how through the day, it does get me

through,

Her smile, if only she knew how it lifts my spirits,

When I'm feeling down or the day is the shits,

Her smile, seeing her smile puts a smile on my

face,

Her smile makes my heart race,

Her smile lights up the place,

Her smile so radiant,

Her smile, my favourite,

Her smile, my happiness,

Her smile, just gorgeous,

Her smile, each one I dearly treasure,

Her smile, each one loved in equal measure,

Her smile, I hope she always has one saved for

me,

Her smile, I hope that I can still be the reason she

smiles occasionally,

Her smile, I hope she has a smile because of this,

Her smile, I hope this book makes her smile, that

is my wish,

Her smile, I hope she never ever loses it,

Her smile, without it, my world, the whole world

would be s%$t.

Her smile, I'll do anything to keep her smiling

and happy,

Her smile, seeing her smile is all that matters to

me and everything to me.

So keep smiling and never lose that sweet,

beautiful, bright smile Khadijah,

Please, I beg ya!

The Voice Of An Angel

No. 44

Khadijah, I guess this poem is a thank you and an apology. I'll explain …

I remember that afternoon, when I was walking past your office, I wasn't sure if I was meant to hear, but you were humming and singing, it was such a beautiful, soft, sweet, angelic sound and mate, I'm not just saying that, it was, it was really beautiful, you were like a little delicate songbird, it was lovely to hear, it made me smile and feel all warm and lovely inside, it brightened my afternoon hearing a sound so sweet, so lovely, so beautiful.

I didn't come into your room or disturb you, just listened for a second or two and went back to my desk. I did text you apologising saying I'm not sure if I was meant to hear but just wanted to say your voice is beautiful, I heard you singing and humming and you have a beautiful voice. Sorry if I wasn't meant to hear but just wanted you to know, you have a beautiful voice.

You sounded horrified, texting back Oh my God, what was I humming and singing? You said you hated your voice and even called it disgusting. I said I wasn't sure what exact tune it was as I didn't stay around listening but that it was a beautiful voice. You sounded so lovely. You made me smile and brightened my afternoon up.

So yeah, matey, apologies again if I wasn't meant to hear but also thank you for making me smile and brightening that afternoon for me and seriously mate, I'm not being bias when I say your voice is beautiful, it really was, it is, I know because of what you think of your voice there is probably no chance of another performance, not even a private concert for your old buddy huh? Not even for Jack? No but seriously, thank you for brightening that afternoon up and making me smile. I guess this was one of them occasions when you made me smile without even knowing you did or meaning to. You make me smile all the time buddy, you're amazing like that!

Sorry and thanks again buddy.

Walking past your office one afternoon,

Coming from your room,

I heard the most beautiful, sweetest tune,

You were humming and singing,

It was spine tingling,

Amazing,

And mesmerising,

205

The sweetest sound I've ever heard,

But you, I didn't disturb,

Instead I listened to you, you were just like a little

songbird,

I listened only for a second,

But, oh what a sweet sound,

Your voice so sweet and lovely,

It sounded so heavenly,

I had to check I was still breathing,

Check I hadn't died and was now in Heaven

residing,

A sound so beautiful that it could be anything

other than heavenly took some believing,

If I had to guess,

Then I guess heaven would sound something like

this,

The voice of an Angel,

So beautiful and sweet was your voice, that you I

simply had to tell,

So when I got back to my desk,

You I did text,

As I said I hope you don't mind me saying,

But I couldn't help listening,

But I heard you humming and singing,

Your voice is so beautiful,

You sounded just like an Angel,

You said "Oh my God", what was I was

humming or singing?

I said I wasn't sure but I loved what I was

hearing,

I didn't stop around long, listening,

I wasn't sure I was meant to hear,

But it was music to my ear,

You said you hated your voice calling it

disgusting,

I said it was beautiful, soft and sweet sounding,

A sound I'd never tire of hearing,

I thanked you anyway for making me smile and

brightening up my afternoon,

With your sweet, angelic, beautiful tune,

I'd love to hear you hum or sing again soon,

But I know because you don't like the sound of

your voice, there is no chance,

Of another performance,

It's a pity,

Not even for me,

Jack, your buddy,

But no seriously,

Mate,

Your voice, you, were great!

Important

No. 45

Khadijah, just a short poem about how in my life you are so important.

I know I haven't known you for long in terms of time, but I feel like I've known you forever, it's a special feeling, I feel like that because I feel like I can talk to you about anything and everything, my feelings, my secrets, my inner most thoughts, my personal stuff, you know I struggle or I've told you how I struggle to open up to people, usually it takes me a very long time to trust people with stuff like that, not with you though, it was instant it shows clearly how special you are, how comfortable I am with you, how comfortable you make me feel, you're a special person Khadijah, truly special.

You're so important in my life, I've told you several times I think the world of you which is why you're the first person I want to tell anything and everything too and share things with. You're in the special category, my inner circle of very few trusted persons who I can truly confide in and tell everything to.

I hope you know how special you are matey, and hope this book shows you how you mean the world to me buddy, I'm so lucky to have an amazing friend like you who I trust completely, I hope you know how important you are in my life, to me, I really don't think there is any higher than you matey.

Every night I thank God for you coming into my life, he has truly blessed me with a special person like you I can trust, confide in, share anything and everything with.

To me you're more than just a mere mortal,

You're special,

You're one of my special people,

You're in my inner circle,

To you, it should hopefully be clear,

That to my heart I hold you oh so very near,

To me you're so very dear,

You're so important to me,

In my life you're ranked so highly,

The line, is one that you already knows,

I trust you as Jack said to Rose,

I know I can tell and talk to you about anything,

You're the first person I want to tell everything,

In my life you hold a position of prominence,

To me, you're a special person of such great

importance,

Opening up to people and talking feelings,

emotions etc I find hard,

But not with you, I can be like an open book, I

can open my heart,

That's why I hold you in such high regard,

Khadijah,

Than you I hold no-one higher,

I've told you before,

I'm sure,

But you know, I think the world of you, you

mean everything to me,

So that's why buddy,

I can't think of any greater endorsement,

Than telling you that to me you're so important.

Version

No. 46

Khadijah, I thank you. I thank you for making me want to be a better version of myself, the way you encourage me, the way you give me confidence and support me, the way you always pick me up off the floor when I'm low, the way you always give me advice and give me perspective and a different way of thinking and looking at things in our chats when I confide in you, the way you help me see the positives and ignore the negatives. Have I told you how truly amazing and inspirational you are? You're one in a billion matey. If it wasn't for you ... well you know.

Yes buddy, you make me want to be a better version of me, a better person, the best I can be. I don't want to let you down buddy.

You make me want to be a better person,

Of me, you make me want to be a better version,

To me, you're an inspiration,

You give me a boost in confidence,

With your kind compliments,

And the way you always offer me words of

encouragement,

To be the best me,

To be the best that I can be,

To be a better person,

To be my best version,

For you I strive to be the best that I can be,

For you, I want to give the best of me,

With you in my life you make me a better person,

To you, I want to give you the best version.

You're Just As Good As Them

No. 47

Khadijah, I know I'm one to talk about believing in one's self, I'm my own worst critic as you know, you, however, always gives me support and encouragement and tells me to believe in myself, you've told me before that I'm talented when it comes to writing these poems (hope so, hope you are liking these poems especially written for you) but enough about this idiot, this is about you buddy, you know I'm your biggest fan and believe in you and I am behind you, I know you worry what others think of you that you have worked with in the past and what they might think of you, you being conscious that you are classed as a trainee and "not qualified" but matey, you're just as good as them buddy, just because you haven't got the paper "YET" but you will get it, (just a formality), it doesn't mean they are any better than you, you're brilliant at your job, the client's love you, you're so good with them, you make them feel at ease, you have such a good manner with them and make them feel comfortable and you know what you're doing. I mean you've seen some of the emails and calls we get from "solicitors" on the other side with the titles, "solicitor" after their name and some of the things they say or ask, and they ain't a patch on you matey, some of the stuff we see you gotta ask do the law society just hand these out to anyone? or do they buy them over the internet?, because some of them you wonder how they passed! Probably paid a bribe or something.

Yes so, believe in yourself buddy, believe, because you're amazing, you're clever, you're hard working, you never give up no matter what life has thrown at you, you inspire me, well I've told you that before in our chats and how amazing I think you are, be proud of yourself matey of how far you've come, what you've achieved and you're going to go far matey, nothing is beyond you buddy, as I said you're amazing, inspirational, clever, determined and driven I could go on with the plaudits, the list is endless. You're just as good as them buddy (better if you ask me but I am just more than a little bias) lol.

Don't worry what they think of you,

You're brilliant at what you do,

Yes, they might have the piece of paper,

But it doesn't mean that they're any better,

You're just as good as them bud,

So never ever think you're not as good,

You know I'm bias but in my opinion you're just

as good as them,

And soon you'll have your paper to prove it, not a

case of if but when,

So chin up young lady,

Don't you worry,

Let them think what they want but you're just as

good as them if you ask me,

Be proud of yourself, how far you have come,

And of everything you have done,

You can keep the rest,

For you're the best,

If you ask me, you're number one!

Ten out of ten,

You're just as good as them!

Believe in yourself Khadijah,

I'm proud of and believe in ya!

Somebody Special

No. 48

Khadijah, I'll admit one of the more if not most emotional poems I've done in this book.

You came down to use my computer to do an SDLT, and as we do, we had a chat, I told you I appreciated the company, when you apologised for disturbing me, you said disturbed not me, I told you, you never bother me or disturb me.

We talked about the usual, how we are etc., how the day has been, the answer is of course always busy and with the weekend approaching, weekend plans obviously cropped up. You said most likely you were going to London again but were hoping your brother would go instead of you then it would be time with the nieces and nephews and the usual. You asked me then about mine, and I said oh the usual, the Caravan Park, they have a singer on, you said you'd have to check the caravan park out one of the times and I said you're more than welcome, if you ever fancy it, let me know, I said there is always something on entertainment wise and if you fancy it, I'll pick you up in a taxi, make sure you got home safely and said even bring your Mum if you want to have a girly night out with her. You said you were not sure your Mum would want to but said you would definitely check it out at some point. I said sure, like I say let me know, the offer is always there.

You asked me if there was anyone special at the caravan park. I said no, no there isn't. I said what about you, anyone special? Any Mr Lucky in your life? You said yes, you were seeing a nice guy but it wasn't anything serious. I do recall telling you I hope he realises how lucky he is.

And that's it for the intro, a bit emotional this one so I'll let you read the poem and leave the intro there.

You know I wish you nothing but all the happiness in the world buddy.

Downstairs it was just me,

When briefly,

You came and kept me company,

Whilst you borrowed my computer to do an

S.D.L.T,

I said sure buddy,

As you asked if you could bother me,

I said I told you you're never any bother for me, I

thought you knew,

You remember, anything for you!

You said you won't be long as you said sorry,

I said don't be daft, take as long as you need, you

know I love your company,

So as you was doing that,

We had, as usual, a little chat,

You know the usual, how we are?

The conversation did turn to the weekend as it

wasn't that far,

You said the usual, time with family,

Nieces and nephews to keep me busy,

That was if you didn't have to go to London

again,

You did explain,

Saying you wasn't a fan of driving there as it's a

pain,

Not to mention the travel time, stress and strain,

So instead,

You said,

You were hoping instead, your bro,

Would go,

As you'd been to London quite frequently,

Recently,

You then said what about you?

What you up to?

Any plans?

Me?, I said, the usual, going to the park with the

caravans,

You asked if there was anyone special at the

Caravan Park,

I shook my head and said Nah,

You said it sounds fun,

And that you'll have to check it out sometime,

I said you're more than welcome,

You could bring your Mum,

I said you could sit in the V.I.P area of mine,

I said there is always entertainment be it a singer

or karaoke,

If you fancied it I'd pick you up in a taxi,

And made sure you got home safely,

Come the end of the night, buddy,

You said yeah, at some point, definitely, we'll go,

I said no problem, just let me know,

You said you wasn't so sure if your Mum would

come to be fair,

And I said, well you know she is more than

welcome, the offer is always there,

I said I'd pay for everything,

It wouldn't cost you a thing,

I said on the karaoke, you might even persuade

me to sing!

Whatever you fancied, perhaps even Elvis the

King?

Then it came to me, as I said I got it, wait, wait,

It's gotta be our song by our mate,

Surely,

Our friend Georgey,

George Michael and "Faith", our song we had for

when you was preparing for your exam,

The conversation then turned back to you, as I

asked what about you? Anyone special? Any

special man?

Ooh, forgive me here,

This is where I may get a bit emotional

writing and shed a tear,

Ooh this is where when writing I just find my

heart beginning to race,

I need to take a short break before I continue

this poem and let the heart return to normal

pace,

It happens quite a bit I find,

When some of the memories replay in my

mind,

Anyway, right, I've took a few minutes, so lets

continue with the poem,

Hope after the break, I can still keep the poem

flowing,

So anyway, you said yes,

But said it wasn't serious,

He's a nice guy,

Admittedly inside I did cry,

Admittedly, I felt envious,

I felt jealous,

I thought lucky S.O.B,

As I was green with envy,

But no, I really do hope he makes you happy,

Buddy,

I hope he realises he's so very, very lucky,

He must surely feel like everyday he's won the

lottery,

But no being serious,

You know I wish you nothing but happiness,

You're beautiful,

You're an amazing girl,

You deserve someone special, you deserve to feel

special,

You know I think the world of you and always

will,

You're my amazing friend,

Jack and Rose huh? Until the end!

Beautiful

No. 49

Khadijah, a poem to hopefully give you a confidence boost.

Matey, you know how I always try to encourage you and support you any way I can, and tell you how amazing and great you are, well this is a reminder too.

During our friendship we've had many, many chats, and you'll see from the Jason Statham poem in this book when I touch on that, how he didn't respond to my messages to him and you saying he was probably too busy with his supermodel girlfriend to respond and I said to you if he saw you he'd soon drop her like a bad smell and you said oh stop it, I said it's his loss not responding playing with rocks and missing a diamond like you. You said aww, you're so sweet. Well we've had conversations before where you've run yourself down saying you wished you looked like them or such and such is so pretty ... and then you'd make me laugh by saying "bitch" but it does hurt me seeing you, hearing you do that, because matey, you're beautiful. You are beautiful inside and out, I've told you countless times you're the sweetest, most kindest, most selfless person I've ever met and have the biggest, sweetest heart, how you always put others first. You're amazing matey, truly amazing and you're just as good as them, better in my bias opinion.

I do wish you could see yourself through my eyes and see what a beautiful lady you are.

Anyway I just wanted to say I think you're beautiful matey even if you don't.

Anyway read on and hopefully it boosts your confidence a bit, it's what friends are for matey.
xx

.

It hurts me,

To hear you run yourself down matey,

When you question your own beauty,

When you've compared yourself to other women,

Claiming that they are a better specimen,

When in some of our chit chat,

You've said I wish I looked like that,

You know how I've always tried to big you up,

And tell you, you're more than good enough,

I've always said to you, you're better than them,

you're beautiful too,

You always say aww you're sweet, thank you,

225

bless you, you know like you do,

But oh how I wish you could see yourself through

my eyes,

Oh how you, they would tell no lies,

Khadijah, you're special,

You're stunningly beautiful,

I wish you could see,

Buddy,

To have you, any guy in the world would be so,

so, damn lucky,

It'd be like everyday winning the lottery,

If you ask me,

No-one compares to you matey,

Oh how I wish you saw your own beauty,

You always look so elegant and classy,

Refined and a proper lady,

Your hair,

Always looks nice, whichever way, it, you wear,

That time you wore no make up and was all

natural,

You looked sensational,

You always do,

Like the song, no-one compares to you,

Oh how me,

Does wish you would see,

Buddy,

Your unrivalled beauty,

Khadijah,

No-one compares to ya,

You're special,

You're beautiful,

If you don't believe me matey, then listen to these
music stars Khadijah,

Like "Beautiful" by Christina Aguilera,

Listen to the lyrics, "You are Beautiful in every
way",

That's what I'm trying to say,

Inside and out, you're the most beautiful person
I've ever met with the biggest, sweetest, most
kindest heart of gold,

When they made you matey, they broke the
mould,

Or like the Prince song, "The most beautiful girl
in the world",
Or that other song earlier referred to,
"No-one compares to you",
By Sinead O'Connor,
Khadijah,
Music clearly plays a big part in our friendship as
you can see,
Hopefully this poem gives you a boost in
confidence matey,
And you realise your beauty,
Because as I said earlier Khadijah, you're special,
You're beautiful.

I'll Always Remember You

No. 50

Khadijah, you know this because I've told you many times in our chats how I think the world of you and cherish every second in your company, how I love our chats and conversations from the serious, heavy stuff to the small things like the weather or something, I remember and cherish them all.

I've said that even if we drift apart and I hope we never do but if we should, know and I have told you, but please know, that I would never ever forget you and would always appreciate the times spent together, the games we play when we go into the town at dinner time and sit on our bench, people walking past probably think I'm Forrest Gump or something rambling to a random pretty lady sitting on the bench next to me just trying to mind her own business and eat her lunch not believing someone like you would be talking to me! Lol. But no, we've had some laughs and fun and I've loved every second of it.

I'll never forget how you can always make me smile and laugh by not even doing anything particular, I just find I smile whenever I'm around you, I've said a million times how you are the sunshine on a dark day, I've told you before how it could be pissing with rain outside

229

but in my world with you around, in your presence, I'm basking in permanent sunshine!

I'll never forget the sound of your voice as gentle and soft as the warm summer breeze, the sound of your sweet infectious laughter, hearing your laugh always makes me smile and laugh I just love your laugh, something about it just unexplainably makes me happy, makes me smile, makes me laugh. I'll never forget the sound of your voice, you make me laugh with your brilliant accents that you do and put on, the way you bless me with your "Aww bless ya", I read some of our old texts and it's like I can hear your voice saying it, no, I won't forget that either, I won't ever forget you matey, the most loveliest, sweetest, most amazing human I've ever met I've told you before how you've got the most sweetest, most biggest heart of anyone I've ever met, you're the most selfless person I've ever met, always putting others first above yourself, including me, when you've always been there for me and got me through some stuff I wouldn't have made it through if not for you, so thank you again buddy. Like I've said buddy, you're important too so make sure you do and try to take time for yourself because you matter too, you matter oh so much, and know, I'll be here for you should you ever need me/someone, anytime, any place. You've got so much on yourself with your own stuff but yet always put others first, you're bloody amazing, do you know that buddy? I'll never forget what you've done for me, how you've been there,

230

how you just seem to know when I'm not myself and you've gone out your way giving your valuable time, time that you won't get back just to check if I was ok, you're bloody wonderful you are!

Anyway, you get the gist, I guess what I'm saying is that if we ever drift apart, just know I'll never forget you, I'll always remember you Khadijah and maybe if we did ever drift apart, I don't know, that maybe just occasionally you may think of something and remember me, for arguments sake say you watched Titanic and you saw Jack and Rose, maybe you'd see it and remember this idiot here and say I remember our Jack and Rose thingy majig and smile.

I'll forever,

Remember,

Never will I forget you,

The most beautiful, sweetest, bright, amazing, girl

I ever knew,

Yes, I'll always remember you,

And all the memories and moments we shared

too,

Whatever style or however you wear it,

It always looks perfect,

I refer to your beautiful golden blonde hair,

The warm sweet, cute, sexy, bright smile that you
wear,

The sound of your voice and the sound of your
infectious laughter,

You know how your smile and your laugh always
brightens my day,

But anyway,

Then, now and forever,

You I'll always remember,

Even if we ever drift apart,

Khadijah, buddy, wherever I may be,

Rest assured you'll always be with me,

As I'll carry you in my heart.,

In life rarely do we get to meet people so special,

but you are, and for that reason life has been a
pleasure,

Meeting you and having the honour of being your
friend, I'll forever treasure,

Yes, you dear Khadijah, I'll always remember,

The cherished memories of our chats and time

spent together,

I'll never let go,

Yes it's a quote, Jack and Rose, I know!

Here it comes, another thank ya, Khadijah,

I'll never ever forget ya!

Sentimental

No. 51

Khadijah, I told you before in one of our many chats that I'm eternally grateful for all the beautiful, magical moments spent in your company, the chats, the laughs, the tears (the tears are mainly this softies) you know I get emotional because I care about you deeply and cherish every second spent in your company, I don't know why but around you, with you, I just feel so damn happy, I can't stop smiling, I've told you before how you are always my favourite part of the day, how you brighten up my day, my world, my life by just being in it, you are always that sunshine buddy! Oh how you've got me through some storms.

And yeah, I guess I am a sentimental fool, I cherish every moment with you and save each precious memory in the memory bank, often replaying them and smiling. I try to remember everything from our conversations to everything really, I always listen intently to whatever you say because I care, because I'm interested because you matter, I've told you before you could read the phone book and I'd remember it, hey maybe we could try that as a talent on Britain's Got Talent or something. Lol Sometimes I read our old texts and smile like an idiot.

I guess what I want to say or are trying to say is thank you, thank you for every second spent in your company, I cherish every one, I cherish every precious memory and I hope we have many, many, more moments together, many more laughs, maybe not so many tears though eh? You did make me smile recently when you said we'll have more memories together and I hope so, I really hope so buddy.

Anyway, this sentimental fool just wanted to say thanks for doing me the honour of allowing me to spend time in your company and making me smile, making me happy, making me feel special.

As I've told you before, I so hope we never drift apart but should we ever, then I want you to know, I'll never ever forget you or the beautiful, precious, cherished moments spent in your company matey. Thank you. I'll remember them forever, I'll remember you forever, the most sweetest, kindest, most amazing, most special person, I've ever, ever met, with the biggest, sweetest, most kindest heart always putting others first, when you need to remember that you are important too, you bloody are to me buddy!

Mark. X (A.K.A. Jack)

Sentimental me,

Holding on to each memory,

235

As through the pages of my memory bank I trawl,

Each precious moment spent with you I recall,

As I dearly cling on to them all,

Unable to delete and let them go,

And so,

In my mind I replay them over and over,

Memories of you and I, Khadijah,

Memories of the times we've spent together,

Memories I'll forget never,

All the conversations we've had are in there,

Memories of the beautiful, bright, sweet smile

that you wear,

Memories of the times together that we did share,

Looking back I get emotional,

As I get all sentimental,

Looking back on each cherished moment,

And the time in your company that I spent,

I look back fondly,

On those special magical times spent with thee,

Those moments and memories I hold so very

dearly,

Try as I may,

I just can't bring myself to let these feelings and

memories fade away,

To me they're just too precious,

Those memories saved under "us",

I confess,

I'm just a sentimental fool I guess.

THE LAST WORD

Well, Khadijah, there we have it buddy, we've reached
the end of the book.

I hope you enjoyed reading it, I hope you smiled, I
hope you laughed along the way and not too many
tears shed I hope.

I know since I finished this collection we have
probably made more memories and had more things
that I could write a poem about, who knows maybe a
sequel in the future I hope.

Anyway I'll keep the final word short and perhaps the
final word or words should be "Thank You".

Thank you for everything Khadijah, the laughs, the
memories, the magic moments spent with you,
everything just everything.

I hope the book says it all, I hope it says thank you to
ya! I hope it makes you feel special and appreciated,
because you are, I am eternally grateful for your
friendship buddy, I am so lucky and blessed to have a
friend like you matey.

You are wonderful and amazing.

And with that said, my dear, beautiful and amazing friend, I guess I will just leave the final words as "Thank You".

Love Mark (A.K.A Jack) xx

Printed in Great Britain
by Amazon

29905645R10136